No Sacrifice Too Great

NO SACRIFICE TOO GREAT

THE STORY OF ERNEST AND RUTH PRESSWOOD

Ruth Presswood Hutchins

Christian Publications

CAMP HILL, PENNSYLVANIA

Christian Publications
3825 Hartzdale Drive, Camp Hill, PA 17011

The mark of ⊕ *vibrant faith*

ISBN: 0-87509-512-7
LOC Catalog Card Number: 93-70742
© 1993 by Christian Publications

93 94 95 96 97 5 4 3 2 1

Unless otherwise indicated, Scripture taken from the King
James Version of the Bible.

Dedication

To The Christian and Missionary Alliance
missionaries who have faithfully
carried the torch proclaiming
the gospel of Jesus Christ
throughout the islands
of Indonesia

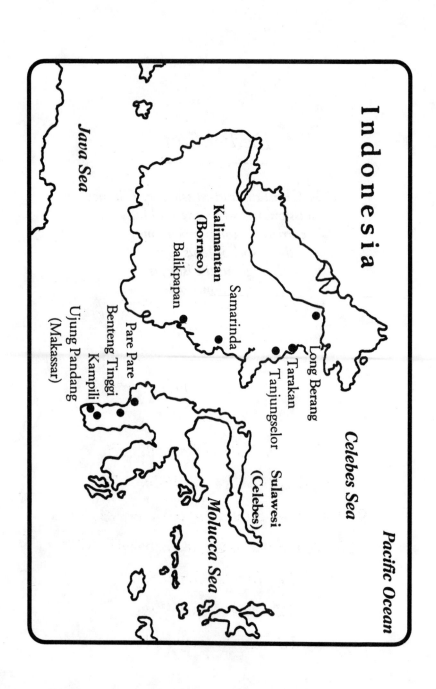

Contents

Acknowledgments

I would like to express my thanks and appreciation to the following:

The editors of the Indonesian *Pioneer* and *Alliance Life* magazines who gave permission to reprint articles by Rev. W.E. Presswood and Rev. P.J. Luijendijk;

Martha Jean, my daughter, who typed, advised and placed my story onto computer;

Larry, her husband, who has exercised patience and endurance through the years of this writing;

The Cheerio Kids—Stephanie and Jimmy—my grandchildren, who have been great encouragers;

All friends and family who persuaded me to keep on writing until the story was finished;

Lillian and Violet, for letters and Presswood family information;

Muriel, for the preliminary editing of my manuscript;

Joyce, who introduced me to Marilynne, who has been a kind and helpful editor.

The names of places used throughout the book are those that were in use at the time the events occurred. The Netherlands East Indies is now called The Republic of Indonesia. Makassar is now Ujung Pandung. Celebes Island is now called

Sulawesi and Borneo is Kalimantan. The spellings of other words have for the most part been changed into contemporary usage.

Preface

In 1970, to fulfill the request of Rev. J.C. Pollock, an author from England, I wrote at considerable length about the life and ministry of Ernest Presswood. At that time, a conviction came upon me that I had a story to be told, a story that had taken me 20 years to forget.

I began to pray about the matter. The task seemed too great for me.

Now, it has taken me another 20 years to remember, and to research, organize and write this book.

These pages contain the story of my life, especially the years in the Netherlands East Indies as the wife of the pioneer missionary, William Ernest Presswood. Those years included internment by the Japanese during World War II and the tragedy of its aftermath.

It was during those trials and testings, when the sacrifice seemed too great, that I took courage in God's Word that the "trial of [my] faith, being much more precious than of gold that perisheth, though it be tried with fire" would, at the coming of Christ, be found to His praise and His honor and His glory (1 Peter 1:7).

That is still my prayer.

1

Benteng Tinggi

"I will say of the LORD, He is my refuge and
my fortress: my God; in him will I trust."
(Psalm 91:2)

Friday the 13th, the 13th of March, 1942. The date is etched in my mind forever. The day began as usual—rising at 6 a.m., eating breakfast with my husband, Ernie, and each of us going about our regular business—he to counsel and teach the believers who had fled the city to the haven of the large conference building at the top of the hill—and me, to my language study.

Ernie always returned about noon. I could count on that.

Suddenly, however, just moments after leaving, Ernie burst through the bedroom door.

"The Japanese are here. I have five minutes to get ready."

"Get ready for what?" I asked, trying to mask an uninvited stab of fear with monotone consistency.

"They are taking the men to Makassar to be examined. At least that is what they say." Ernie pulled open a drawer and reached in.

4

With few words passing between us, we collected a change of clothing, a toothbrush, a shaving kit, a notebook and a special pen with ink in one end and a pencil in the other. It was mine, but I wanted Ernie to have it.

Ernie reached for my Bible.

"I will take your Bible because it is smaller than mine," he explained.

With the little black suitcase finally packed, we embraced.

"The Lord be with you, my dear," he said. "They say we are coming back soon."

Ernie hurried out the door and up the mountain path to the truck where the Japanese were waiting. I followed him as far as I dared, a deepening shadow of apprehension crowding slowly but surely into my soul.

Russell, a missionary colleague, was already on the truck. Darlene, his wife, stood alone at a distance. I joined her and in silence we watched the truck bump down the lane and onto the narrow road below the compound.

"God," I prayed, "in Jesus' name, help me to be strong."

Ernie and I had been married one year and three months and, in fact, I had been on this beautiful island in the East Indies less than eight months.

Was this the end of our dreams? Was a missionary career that had hardly begun about to end in tragedy? Would Ernie and I ever see each other again? Question after question begged for an answer.

But at that moment, there were none.

Since the turn of the century, the Japanese had desperately pursued ways and means to gain more land and power. Particularly after World War I they were convinced that they deserved greater recognition as a world power.

Believing that the United States was a threat to the trading of resources to Eastern Asia, in 1921 Japan took over the region of Manchuria, adding it to her already expanding collection of Pacific Islands that had formerly been owned by Germany. These she used to fortify her position and invade China.

In November of 1941, Japanese diplomats arrived in Washington, D.C. to talk peace. At the very same time, Japanese aircraft carriers were already on their way across the Pacific to position themselves for an attack on Hawaii.

The tragic day arrived—Pearl Harbor was bombed. The United States and its allies, already preoccupied with a bloody war in Europe, were now forced into another war arena, this one with Japan.

From that time on, Japan attacked island after island, by land, sea and air. Drunk with victory, they swept through Guam, Midway, Wake Island, the Philippines, Borneo and Hong Kong.

December 17, 1941, found them in Borneo. January 2, 1942, they occupied Manila in the Philippines. February 4th, they demanded the unconditional surrender of Singapore. February 9th, they landed on the Celebes Island. These areas could supply the oil and raw materials that Japan needed.

Makassar had been our home, but the ominous

news crackling over our radio, along with the tropical heat, had prompted 10 missionaries, including ourselves, to head for Benteng Tinggi, a beautiful, somewhat secluded mountain resort where we could, in comfort, wait out whatever might happen.

Our group included Dr. Robert Jaffray, his wife Minnie, their daughter Margaret, three single missionaries—Lilian Marsh, Margaret Kemp, Philoma Seely—and two couples—Russell and Darlene Deibler and Ernie and me.

Now, with Russell and Ernie gone, just eight of us were left. Dr. Jaffray had been spared the ordeal because of the Japanese respect for white hair. They also thought he took too many medicines because of the many bottles on the dresser in his bedroom. Actually, they were cologne bottles.

As darkness fell that Friday the 13th night, eight people gathered at the Jaffray residence. None of us was very talkative that evening, each one consumed with his or her own thoughts, questions, memories.

Yes, memories.

I thought of my happy-go-lucky childhood days in Albion, New York. A family of nine children was a real houseful. I often wondered how my mother remained so calm, for eight of those children were boys. I was the only girl, the second-born child.

What a gang we were! We had no television. We didn't even have a radio. But we didn't need a lot of outside entertainment—we made our own.

Even though we were carefree, life was quite regimented. Mother and Dad's word was law. If we were told to do something, our parents expected their orders to be carried out. They might remind us once; after that, we suffered the consequences.

We all had our jobs to do. One of mine was to see that my brothers washed their faces and hands and combed their hair before sitting down at the table to eat.

The dining room table was the common meeting place. It was a big, solid oak, oval table with four elephant-type legs. As the family grew, so did the table. It eventually boasted six large leaves. Dad sat in the middle with the two youngest boys on each side of him. I sat across from Dad, Mother sat at the end by the kitchen door and the boys sat between. The order never changed.

We were all supposed to make our beds. With the boys, that got a little complicated because they slept two to a bed. Mother would say, "Have you made your bed?" Often the answer was, "I made my side!"

There was always lots of work, very hard work. Even though Dad had hired help and a "year man" in the tenant house, there never seemed to be enough workers. My duties were in the house doing "women's work." Since I was the only girl, my mother and father were determined that I remain "feminine."

In the summer of 1917, the measles swept through our town. We attended a school picnic where it was "going around," and one by one our whole family succumbed. I especially remember Pete. When Pete began to feel sick, he went out and picked a bouquet of flowers, put it on his dresser, then went to bed!

Everyone was concerned about Mother. She was expecting another baby and she had never had the measles. The dreaded thing happened—Mother contracted the disease. However, on September 23rd, she gave birth on schedule to a normal, healthy baby. She named him Robert. About three weeks later, baby Robert contracted the measles, too.

Our large, wood frame farmhouse was flanked on either side by two tall pine trees. One of them sported a rope swing. To the right of the driveway were two big maple trees which we tapped for sap in the spring to make maple syrup. There were also English walnut trees which never bore many nuts, but provided good shade and low branches which became our acrobat bars.

The one-room, cobblestone schoolhouse was just one mile from our home in the village of Fairhaven (now called Childs). Every day, in all kinds of weather, we walked the mile to and from school proudly carrying our lunch boxes and books.

Each morning we pledged allegiance to the American flag. We sang "My Country 'Tis of Thee" and "The Star-Spangled Banner." Our spirits were high because this was war time—the First World War.

Ah, war. What an odious word! It was war that had sequestered us here in Benteng Tinggi, virtual prisoners at our own denominational retreat center. Although the surroundings were beautiful and the accommodations commodious, all 10 of us would much rather have been elsewhere.

Ernie and I had been in the city of Makassar on

the island of Celebes only five months before the alarming news of the bombing of Pearl Harbor had come.

The 1941 senior class of the Bible school there had had its graduation. The graduates had been counseled on how to proceed because of the war and some were given assignments to strategic places of ministry. Trip after trip had been made to the harbor as the missionaries tried to contact boats, ships or anything traveling to other islands that could help evacuate the Christians from Makassar.

Now the question was: what would the missionaries do?

The Japanese were advancing at an alarming rate through the Philippines, the China Sea, Celebes Sea and Makassar Straits, conquering each island as they advanced. Rumors were that they were killing ruthlessly, especially on the island of Borneo.

Where were we to go? What did the Lord have in mind for us? Time was fast running out for those of us in the Celebes Island. One day Ernie came home with bad news.

"According to the officials," he said, "any one or all of the ladies should evacuate to Java, the United States, Canada or wherever they can get transportation."

Ernie asked me if I wanted to go.

"No, I don't think so," I responded rather hesitatingly as my eyes focused on my husband of less than one year, "especially if you are not going."

His response was immediate: he and Russell had decided to stay.

The days that followed were filled with prayer, reading the Word and singing hymns. It was becoming clear then, if it hadn't been before, that nothing was going to be easy. Either choice—to go or to stay—could mean death. Later we heard that a ship transporting evacuees had been torpedoed and all lives had been lost. We could have been on that ship.

God had given me a special verse several years before when I had set my mind toward the mission field. It was Philippians 4:13: "I can do all things through Christ which strengtheneth me." The "all things" I needed strength to meet were now becoming an everyday occurrence. The chorus of the song, "Precious Hiding Place," gave me courage:

> Precious hiding place,
> Precious hiding place,
> In the shelter of His love.
> Not a doubt nor fear
> Since my Lord is near,
> And I'm sheltered in His love.

That hiding place, that place of shelter, would come to mean more to me than I could ever know at that moment.

Each one of the missionary women was faced with the same decision, whether to go or stay. Margaret Kemp said that she was willing to leave and take Mrs. Jaffray, who was now 70 years old, with her. But it was too late. When they tried to make travel arrangements, no transportation was available.

So everyone stayed and prepared for war, trying to make the best of the deteriorating conditions. We made air raid shelters, but they filled up with water. A vacant lot next to our house was turned into a training grounds for Dutch Indonesian soldiers. Later, sharpened bamboo stumps, four or five feet high, were pounded into the ground. They were intended to injure or kill anyone who would dare to parachute into the area.

The bellowing alarm of the first air raid sounded one day when I was alone in downtown Makassar shopping for a present for Ernie's birthday. Fortunately I had already made my purchase—a genuine crocodile skin wallet—and was on my way home in a tiga roda (a three-wheeled bicycle or pedicab). The man who was pedaling the vehicle pulled to the side of the street as the alarm blared. We sat motionless until the "all clear" came.

War or no war, I wanted to make Ernie's birthday as special as possible. I decided to make him a cake. Of course, we had no cake mixes—it had to be made from scratch. Neither was there any vanilla extract, and I knew that a white cake with white frosting certainly needed vanilla. Bet, my house helper, gave me some raw substance from the vanilla bean. I added a generous portion.

The finished cake looked nice, but, oh, the taste! The vanilla flavor was so strong that we couldn't even eat a bite of it! I should have known that raw spices from the spice islands were very different from those in North American bottles or cans!

Dr. and Mrs. Jaffray, their daughter, Margaret, and the other other women left for Benteng Tinggi after the Bible school graduation. Darlene and I stayed with our husbands as long as we felt safe. However, on January 21st, we were driven to Benteng Tinggi in the Jaffrays' car. The car and driver returned to Makassar.

Russell (the assistant field chairman) and Ernie (who had accepted the responsibility of Bible school principal) remained in Makassar to stock up on supplies for the months ahead at Benteng Tinggi. Ernie and Russell had been classmates at Nyack Missionary Training Institute and now they were ministering together far from American shores, blissfully unaware of the experiences they would share in the days ahead. For now, our team was just looking forward to some "R and R" in the cool, mountain air.

When the Japanese made their landing on the island, Ernie and Russell escaped in the Jaffrays' car, joining the rest of us in Benteng Tinggi in the middle of the night of February 2nd.

2

Not So Easy to Die

"Thou therefore endure hardness,
as a good soldier of Jesus Christ."
(2 Timothy 2:3)

Benteng Tinggi, located 3,000 feet above sea level, means "tall fort," a name which seemed particularly appropriate given the situation in the area at this time. Benteng Tinggi was the site of the annual Christian and Missionary Alliance conference. The missionaries always looked forward both to the warm fellowship and cool air. Just to be there on the mountains was refreshing in every way.

Two fair-sized houses adorned the Mission property which had been leased from the Dutch government. One house was owned by the Jaffrays and the other by Lilian Marsh. The conference house and a few small buildings were up the hill from Lilian's house. Our Bible school students and other Christian nationals lived in those buildings.

The view of the velvet green mountains across the valley with their terraced, irrigated rice fields was a sight to behold. We were so far above sea level that the clouds actually floated through the open windows. The Lord was good to give us this beautiful spot. In addition to the missionaries now sequestered here, there were many national Christians. It was a colony of perplexed, frightened people.

At first Ernie and I and the Deiblers occupied the two guest rooms in the Pavilion, which was the house owned by the Jaffrays. The Pavilion guest rooms were attached to the main house by a covered walkway and included a bathroom equipped for "dipper" showering.

One morning at the crack of dawn, a knock came on our door. It was Margaret Jaffray.

"Ruth," she gasped breathlessly, "will you come and help the family down the hill? The wife has been in labor all night. The baby's feet are coming first. They are saying that this is bad because the mother and baby always die."

"I will be there as soon as possible," I said, hurrying off to get dressed. "Boil some water and bring towels, basins and some soap."

We hurried down the hill with our meager medical supplies. Arriving at the small, thatched-roof bamboo shack, I walked up the steps and peeked in the door. All was dark. There were no windows. The ceiling was so low that it was impossible for me to stand up. I managed to focus on the patient stretched out on a floor about 12 inches higher than the entry level.

My nursing career to this date had certainly not known the confines of such surroundings as these. My mind pictured, as if unbidden, the events that had led me to find myself in the jungles of the East Indies.

There were two Brooks families living in Albion—my own family and my paternal grandparents. To distinguish between the two families, Grandma and Grandpa were known as "The Brookses on the Avenue" and we were known as "The Brookses on the Ridge." In other words, the town Brookses and the country Brookses.

It was especially enjoyable to stay with Grandma on weekends because she attended the Baptist church on Sunday. I liked to go with her. While we lived on the farm, our family seldom went to church. Some of my aunts, uncles, cousins and high school girlfriends did. I remember feeling that it was the right thing to do.

One particular Sunday morning, I was sitting as usual with Grandma in her pew, the fourth from the front on the right hand side. The minister asked if anyone would like to receive Jesus Christ as personal Savior. If so, that person was to come forward and stand at the front. I wanted to go, but I was too timid to respond. The meeting closed and we went home.

Throughout the afternoon hours my mind returned to the service and what the preacher had said.

That evening, Grandma didn't go to church, but she gave me permission to go. This time I sat in one of the rear pews. Again, the invitation was given at the close of the message. However, this time the minister explained that there were cards in the pew rack that could be signed by anyone who wanted to accept Jesus Christ as Savior. I signed one of the cards and put it in the offering plate.

A few days later the minister, with two official men of the church, came to visit Grandma and me. They wanted to make sure I was ready for such a decision. They asked many questions, most of which I did not understand.

The only things I knew about the gospel at that time came from the songs we sang: "Tell Me the Story of Jesus," "Take Time to Be Holy," "When I Survey the Wondrous Cross," "The Old Rugged Cross," "Calling Today" and others. Nevertheless, I had certain basic spiritual desires. I wanted Jesus in my life. I wanted to be baptized. And I wanted to go to heaven some day.

The church accepted me. On April 17, 1927, at the age of 16, I was baptized by immersion. It was a very special occasion. Dad and Mother came to the service. On the way home, with the family loaded into the old Ford, I asked Dad, "Did I say 'I do' okay?" His response was silence. I understood. The Brookses in general were not very communicative at such times and about such things.

The Great Depression in the late '20s hit us hard. Unemployment abounded. People were losing their farms, especially those who did not have them paid for and had to make both mortgage and tax payments. My parents lost their 101-acre farm with the two houses on it. We had an auction, selling farm implements, machinery and animals in order to pay off the debts. It was a bitter pill to swallow.

I greatly admired my mother. She wanted me to

achieve something in life unhindered. Aunt Gertrude also encouraged me by suggesting that I enter Buffalo City Hospital for nurses' training. I decided to take her advice.

Saying goodbye was like a funeral for everyone. My youngest brothers were only three and one respectively. My father had been injured while cutting wood with a buzz saw and it was hard to leave him. I also had a boyfriend to be separated from. All in all, it was a sad occasion. I was finding that it was not easy to part from those you love.

Many other girls were standing around the nurses' home waiting for room assignments when I arrived. I wondered to myself which ones would become my friends and who would be my roommate.

Two girls caught my eye. I thought to myself, *They seem like girls my grandmother would like me to know.*

When I finally received my room assignment, I found out that I had not one roommate, but five! Two of them were the girls my grandmother would have liked—Lillian and Violet Presswood, twins from Toronto, Canada.

Our first night together, with all the girls looking on, Lillian and Violet knelt down at their beds to pray. Impressed (and maybe somewhat convicted), I dropped to my knees, too. It was a good beginning. Not only had we made a statement concerning our faith, but Violet and Lillian and I became life-long friends.

Lillian and Violet attended a Christian and Missionary Alliance church within walking distance of the hospital. Although they belonged to that denomination in Toronto, it was my first introduction to it. The people and their pastor, the Rev. L.J. Isch, welcomed us with open arms. We were often invited to the homes of the congregation for meals and fellowship.

We hadn't been in training very long when Lillian and Violet began talking about their brother, Ernie. He and another young man, Russell Deibler, they said, were preparing to leave soon for Borneo, East Indies. That any young person would want to "waste" his or her life like that was, to my mind, beyond comprehension.

I found nurses' training physically, mentally and emotionally taxing. And so it was a great relief when the initial probation period of four months was over. We were given more privileges, and, best of all, the hospital paid us $15.00 per month and furnished our uniforms and food.

The Lord wonderfully revealed Himself to me in those days at the hospital. My heart and mind were hungry for the truth in God's Word. It gave me strength I had never known before. I learned to pray and to believe that God heard me.

The first big answer to prayer was deliverance from homesickness. After several weeks I was finally able to stop crying myself to sleep each night. What a blessing! And what's more, my purposes and attitudes changed. In fact, my whole life changed radically.

Graduation time came, a time to say goodbye to my friends. We had been through many experiences together. Now we would be away from the shelter of the hospital, out on our own, in a society ravaged by the Great Depression.

Lillian and Violet Presswood returned home to Toronto and found work. Since the distance between Toronto and Buffalo was only about 90 miles, we visited one another often.

Our family doctor, Ralph Brodie, informed me that public health nurses were being hired in Buffalo by the Visiting Nurses Associaton on Franklin Street. He recommended that I apply. I was hired.

Yes, nursing in the thick jungles of a faraway tropical island was much different than visiting the sick in the homes of Buffalo, New York. Trying to adjust my eyes to the darkness of the hut, I began to examine the patient. Her condition was indeed critical. The baby was breach, with one cold leg already dangling out. A breach birth in this primitive situation was more than I could handle. God would need to come to my aid.

With little room inside the hut, Margaret stayed outside to pray. I, too, was pleading for God's intervention as I reached in for the other leg. I was able to manipulate the baby's body enough to allow for delivery. The child was stillborn. We tried to revive the baby, but to no avail. It had been in that critical position too long.

The mother seemed to be all right. In fact, I think she recovered from the delivery more rapidly than I did. I had been in a squatting position for about an hour—wearing a girdle! Dizzy and feeling faint, I stood up and went outside. That was the last time I wore that girdle!

The next day, the family took the patient down the mountain side to a cave. They were afraid the

Japanese would come and find them with white people.

A plantar's wart on the ball of my left foot was causing me a lot of discomfort. To be prepared if the Japanese ordered us on a long march, I decided to try to get help for the foot at a Dutch clinic in the little town of Malino, about one kilometer distant from Benteng Tinggi. Many Dutch women and children had been evacuated to Malino and Dutch police had been assigned for their protection.

Ernie and I chose to walk over a mountain path rather than along the road. One never knew when the Japanese would appear.

We waited in line for some time to see the lady doctor. When my turn came, she applied a boric acid ointment on a patch on the ball of my foot. That was all. Ernie and I both knew that a cure was not likely with such a simple procedure.

We decided to take things into our own hands. Ernie asked Margaret Kemp for some hydrochloric acid which she took regularly for stomach trouble.

Sure enough, with prayer and the acid, the wart was soon eaten away, but so was a part of my foot. A hole the size of a finger nail remained. However, about 10 days later, I exclaimed, "Look, Ernie! My foot is healed!" The hole was gone!

Shortly after the foot episode, an air raid warning sounded over the mountains. All 10 of us crowded into a shelter which had been built in the side of the mountain beside the Jaffrays' house. It was our first alert. We did not know what to expect.

As soon as we had settled into place in the bunker, Mrs. Jaffray started reciting the 91st Psalm in her clear, deep voice. "He that dwelleth in the secret place of the most High shall abide under the shadow of the Almighty." How comforting it was to hear God's Word. We stayed in the shelter about 45 minutes, until the all clear was sounded.

The reason for the air raid warning, we soon found out, was that Malino had been bombed and officially taken over by the Japanese. That was not good news for us, the residents of nearby Benteng Tinggi.

Rumors spread like wildfire, replete with stories of the soldiers' cruelty as they confiscated or destroyed anything and everything they wanted. It was reported that women were raped, even those in hospital beds.

Our turn was not long in coming. What the Japanese expected to find at Benteng Tinggi we'll never know. But they came with a vengeance. A band of soldiers, armed with guns and bayonets, surrounded Lilian's house. Other soldiers swept through the rest of the homes, trying to corral all 10 of us into one small area. An officer rounded up the Jaffrays and the Deiblers from the other house across the ravine. We were lined up in a single-file circle. It wasn't exactly a prayer circle, but one thing was certain—we were all praying.

Ernie was taken into another room. Doing what he thought was appropriate for the occasion, he raised his hands above his head in surrender. This infuriated the soldiers and one of them began to beat unmercifully on his arms. Ernie finally dropped his hands to his sides and the flailing stopped.

As for me, hearing the sounds of the beating and the shouting of the Japanese, I prayed, "Dear Lord, don't let them kill my husband!"

Ernie was brought back into the room and inserted into the circle. I tried to move over to stand by him, but the soldier behind me forced me back in place with the end of his bayonet.

Another soldier strode forward, raised his sheathed sword and began to beat Russell's hands again and again. Russell did not resist. Having already experienced his own beating in the other room, and somewhat the wiser for it, Ernie blurted, "Russell, they want you to put your hands down at your sides."

Russell had been standing in his customary way with his hands in front of him, the palm of one resting on the back of the other. This posture, too, apparently infuriated the Japanese. The maliciousness of the beatings, however, had its desired effect. We all stood motionless, like lambs ready for the slaughter.

"What nationality are you? Where are you from? What are you doing here?" the soldiers asked in staccato fashion. The only place they seemed to know anything about was America.

The Deiblers, Margaret Kemp and Philoma Seely were Americans—the nationality the Japanese hated most. The Jaffrays, Ernie and I were Canadians and traveled on a Canadian passport. (I had dual citizenship because I was married to a Canadian.) Lilian Marsh was from England.

I thought of the last radio newscast we had heard in Makassar.

"I'm here in our building in the center of the city," the reporter had shouted. "The bombs are falling all around us. I'm going to have to close down."

After a moment's hesitation, in desperation he cried, "Come on America!"

At this moment I was sensing his sentiments exactly.

When the inquisition ceased, we were given orders that none of us, under any circumstances, should leave Benteng Tinggi. In other words, we were officially interned and under house arrest.

A sense of relief swept over us as the last truckload of Japanese left. I pinched myself to be sure that I was still alive.

"I didn't expect to be living now," I commented aloud.

Dr. Jaffray responded, "You will find it's not so easy to die."

3

Triumph and Tragedy at Long Berang

"And they overcame him by the blood of the Lamb, and by the word of their testimony; and they loved not their lives unto the death."
(Revelation 12:11)

And now, it was Friday, the 13th—Friday, the 13th of March, 1942. Darlene and I stood watching Ernie and Russell, in the back of the Japanese army truck, going down the lane to the road below. The last sight of them off in the distance at a certain bend on the road to Makassar was their blue shirts blowing in the wind.

Rev. William Ernest Presswood was born in Delaraine, Manitoba, Canada, on January 16, 1908. He was the second of six children, three boys and three girls, with Violet and Lillian, my training roommates, being twins.

The Presswood family moved several times. One of those moves was especially significant in the life of young Ernest. It was while the family was in England that Ernie attended evangelistic meetings conducted by Gypsy Smith. There, at 15 years of age, he accepted Christ as his personal Savior.

Not long afterwards the family returned to Canada, settled in Toronto, and established a meat business. They chose to attend the Christie Street Christian and Missionary Alliance Tabernacle. It was at this church, under the ministry of Oswald J. Smith, that Ernie volunteered his life for missionary service.

As was typical of Ernie, he began immediately to prepare for his future ministry. He enrolled at the Canadian Bible Institute and later at the Missionary Training Institute at Nyack. He graduated in 1929.

Ernie had read Robert A. Jaffray's account of the vision the Lord had given him for Borneo. Through its pages God seemed to kindle a fire in Ernie's heart. Borneo it would be.

With all his needs supplied, Ernie headed west to catch a ship to the Netherlands East Indies. On his way, he stopped in Buffalo, New York, to see Violet and Lillian. That was the first time I met Ernie. In the years that followed, I would hear much more about him.

Arriving in Borneo with him was another young man—Russell Deibler. They joined a missionary staff already in place whose leader was the Rev. Robert A. Jaffray, a man of vision, authority and faith.

Ernie soon found himself deep in the heart of Borneo with the interior Dyaks. Unlike their coastal brothers who were under strong Muslim influence and very resistant to the gospel, the interior

Dyaks showed great interest in the message the white man brought.

In 1932, Ernie wrote:

> *As far as I know, there is not one soul here who knows what it is to be saved. Since coming to this field I have experienced something of the resistance which the great arch enemy of souls makes when his territory has been entered and his so-called rights are called in question. Every season of prayer means a wrestle, every effort to make Christ known brings consciousness of the reality of the conflict.*
>
> *For many centuries these people have been under the bondage and fear of Satan. The fruits he has produced greatly resemble himself: ignorance, superstition, witchcraft, corruption of mind, filth, disease and suffering—these follow in the path of the prince of the power of the air. Only the firm hand of the Dutch keeps the villagers from indulging in the old orgies of head-hunting and tribal warfare. Truly, hate is a very part of the being of Satan. Nevertheless, we feel the Sun of Righteousness is about to rise above this dark picture with healing in His wings.*
>
> *If we could preach to five different villages every week for a year, we could not give every village an opportunity to hear the gospel. A year of ceaseless toil would not cover the field.*

A further report on Ernie's ministry in 1932 appeared in the field missionary magazine, *The Pioneer*:

Everywhere crowds gathered and followed from village to village. The people from tributary streams would assemble at a central place, often 300 at one time. When you realize that the average village in these parts consists of about 40 people, this number is very significant. High mountains, thousands of jungle leeches, slippery hills, muddy swamps, irrigated rice fields—all are natural barriers in this part of the world.

On one occasion, 500 people assembled at the same place. Houses had to be propped up in order to hold the unusual weight. Floors gave way under the strain, while walls had to be knocked out in order to make room for the crowds. Some followed us from village to village in order to hear more of our message. A few of them even followed us for about two weeks. There is no explanation for this except that in answer to the prayers of God's people, His Spirit had been creating a genuine hunger for the gospel.

An insert from page 13 of *The Pioneer* indicated that Ernie had had to return to Makassar for several months in order to allow for an ulcerated foot to heal. After an operation, it took about seven months until he was finally able to return to village ministry. It was a time of soul-searching:

Because He sees our need, even though we fail to, He brings us through all sorts of trials and testings that we may come and learn of Him. Like Martha of old, I was "cumbered about much serving." I was beginning to look upon myself as somewhat indispensable. So the Lord had to teach me that I was not.

Did you notice that I wrote, 'He brings us through all sorts of trials?' He does not leave us in them; He brings us through them.

Again I say that it is great to sit at the Master's feet and learn of Him! I have learned some things that I ought to have learned long ago. Along the line of guidance, I received great light. Also, the work we are engaged in is His. He will clearly reveal each step we should take and supply every need.

Another report, entitled "Advance in Borneo," reveals the cost involved in pioneering that area:

I have just returned from another long trip into the heart of the district of Sesayap in East Borneo. All previous records of my missionary career have been broken—the time involved, the dangers passed through, the opportunities for service, the opposition of the enemy, the taxing of our physical and mental strength, the out-poured blessing of the Lord, the consciousness of His presence, the victories won, and the souls saved.

Just 102 days lapsed from the time we started out on our trip until we reached our station again. Going upstream we encountered high water and at one place were forced to camp high up on the river bank for five nights.

Unfortunately, during our camp-out the carcass of a deer came floating down the river. With extraordinary alacrity, the Dyaks jumped into a dugout, went after the carcass, and in a few moments secured the prize. The deer had been dead several days, but that did not deter the 30 or 40 Dyaks who were camping with us from using it.

The smell beggared description, but no amount of coaxing or scolding prevailed on them to return the deer to the river and the crocodiles. Millions of gnats, not the least bit shy, added to our discomfort.

A couple of days later, when the water was very high and swift, a corpse came floating downstream. We later learned that it was that of a blind child whose father was with us at the time. While the boy had been bathing in the river, the current had proved too strong and had carried him away.

Ernie went on to report 125 baptisms during 33 days of ministry in one area. In another area, some of the national pastors had earlier baptized more than 200 people. After further instruction, deacons were appointed in seven of the villages.

In another area, despite the opposition of the enemy, about 400 more were baptized. Altogether, 946 Dyaks from 67 villages were baptized in that district in three years.

In 1935, Ernie and Russell went home on furlough. Russell had been ministering in a nearby area where the seed had also borne much fruit. *The Pioneer* noted, "These two brethren have labored unstintingly and self-sacrificingly in the interior of Borneo and have endured much hardness as good soldiers of Jesus Christ for the gospel's sake."

Both Ernie and Russell, single during their first term, got married during their first furlough. Ernie married Laura Harmon from Chester, Pennsylvania. Russell married Darlene MacIntire from Boone, Iowa. The two couples spent several months in Holland studying the Dutch language before returning to the Indies.

Ernie and Laura headed toward the interior village of Long Berang. The journey upstream through the rapids during a season of high water was one prolonged nightmare for Laura. In fact, she refused ever to travel the rapids again. Laura was not the first nor the last person who made that decision! Even some of the national teachers' wives chose to live below the 70-mile stretch of horrifying rapids and whirlpools.

Work was going ahead on building the Mission house, but the way was getting tougher, not easier. At times, the building appeared to come to a complete standstill. Laborers left the job, floods washed away lumber that had been prepared and two boats were taken away by the flood waters. Meanwhile, Ernie and Laura lived in a bamboo hut—actually a pig sty—until one room of the house was closed in.

It was 1938. Laura was not well and had a miscarriage. She continued to lose strength. Late at night, on May 6, 1938, Laura passed away, her life taken due to hemorrhaging from the miscarriage. Her body was buried near the house on the side of the hill.

Ernie was left tragically alone. Only national Christians were nearby. Travel and communication

were provokingly slow because both depended on
Dyak men traveling up and down the river and
through the rapids during the rainy season.

Ernie wrote to George Fisk, the nearest missionary, asking him to come and be with him for a
while. George's quick response (quick, at least by
Borneo standards) was much appreciated by Ernie.
He now had someone to share in his grief.

Floods continued that year. The Dyaks said it
was the worst time of flooding in their memory.
They were dark days for Ernie. The desolation of
his soul is revealed in a letter home: "Surely the
Lord does not love me when He treats me thus, I
thought. But He answered me so blessedly, 'Whom
the Lord loveth He chasteneth and so scourgeth
every son whom He receiveth.' Because He loves
me He has caused me to suffer so and not because
He hates me." Somehow, Ernie had the strength to
go on alone.

Later, a young man named John Willfinger was
sent to be his co-worker. John was a pleasant, congenial, understanding companion during the ever-
changing months that followed.

In the summer of 1939, John Willfinger wrote the
following report entitled, "Easter with the Dyaks":

> Over to the left of the mission house lies a trail
> which comes over the mountains from the interior
> and passes right by our door and across the river
> to Long Berang. Since the voices were coming
> from that direction we stood in the mission yard
> and looked out toward the trail.
>
> Gradually the voices became more distinct

and soon we were able to recognize some familiar gospel hymns and my brother's supposition was verified. [Ernie had determined that the sound of voices was not wailing for a deceased Muslim teacher, but of a contingent of Christian Dyaks announcing their arrival by singing.]

It is almost impossible for me to transfer to paper the mixed emotions that throbbed in my breast. At this stage of my term in Borneo, my eyes and ears are constantly on the alert lest I miss some of the new revelations all around me relative to the habits and customs of the people to whom God has called me to minister the unsearchable riches of Jesus Christ.

Shortly afterward, the voices were accompanied by the tramp, tramp, tramp of the feet of this district's regiment of Borneo's Christian army. Keenly and expectantly watching the exit of the trail from the jungle, I was soon confronted by a scene I think I shall not soon forget. Led by the national teachers and evangelists and singing lustily the theme songs of redemption, there came down that narrow trail a long winding line of Dyak men and women marching single file and bearing on their backs baskets of rice—their offering to the risen Lord.

On and on they came until the mission yard became a sea of happy, smiling faces whose charm was added to by the variety of colors in their native dress. Then began a round of almost ceaseless hand-shaking until I thought my arm would become paralytic and refuse to function altogether or else become an automaton and continue of its own accord to move up and down like a pump-handle after the ceremonies had ceased.

But they were real handclasps behind which were grateful hearts that had found in Christ deliverance from sin and superstition. Praise God for these jewels from Borneo, which shall one day adorn the crown of King Jesus. On these faces are no traces of fear and horror, but only joy and peace.

During the rest of the day and the day following the Dyaks kept coming in until we had a large, enthusiastic crowd of happy Christians gathered to worship their risen Lord. Hallelujah!

We had our opening service on Thursday night. About 500 gathered for this service. I had never heard such a great volume of singing in my life before. They sang until it seemed the roof would be raised off the mission house. There was some discord and a little lagging behind on the part of some; but their bright faces and holy enthusiasm more than compensated.

We must bear in mind that a few years ago there was no song in their hearts. But, thank God, wherever Jesus is, there is always a song of joy and gladness, and Borneo is no exception.

Easter Day crowned the great jubilee. By this time about 700 Dyaks had gathered and it reminded me of happy days spent at Mahaffey as the Dyaks milled around the grounds singing and greeting each other warmly. In the morning service we had the administration of Holy Communion and we felt the keen presence of the

Lord. In the afternoon we had the cream of the services in the form of a baptismal service.

Picture this scene. Under the beautiful, clear, tropical sky, with the sunbeams playing on the green calm water of the river, we commence with this holy ordinance, one of the only two that Christ left His church. My heart rejoiced as Brother Presswood and I baptized between us 108 born-again souls in the Name of our risen Lord. Although this was the first Easter spent away from the homeland loved ones, I feel amply recompensed by this glorious season just past. We solicit your earnest prayers that we may glorify Christ here in Borneo.

4

For Such a Time as This

"O God, be merciful unto me:
for my soul trusteth in thee: yea,
in the shadow of thy wings will I make my
refuge, until these calamities be overpast."
(Psalm 57:1)

It was 1940 and Ernie was coming home on furlough.

"At your earliest convenience," the letter read, "I would like to see you."

The letter was no great surprise because ever since Ernie first went to the field, then came home on furlough and married Laura, I had kept in touch with them as members of the Presswood family.

Ernie was the first missionary that I had ever known personally. I had followed him with interest and admiration. It was all new to me in the year 1930 when we first met—how or why someone would go to another country and endure hardships for the sole purpose of preaching the gospel.

We had been exchanging letters often during the

year just preceding his furlough. I knew what this could mean and I began to seek the Lord for guidance concerning His will. I certainly was not going into this blindly even though I was ignorant of missionary life. I reasoned that, if I had the mind of the Lord in the matter, all things would fall into place.

But making the decision was not without its problems. There was another special friend to be considered. My career was at stake, plus I would need additional education. Although I had been working for seven years, I had very little savings. I also knew that there was no one to look to for financial help. The cold facts were that I would have to cash in an insurance policy, sell my car and rent a room instead of an apartment.

About that time, as I was in the valley of decision, I attended a rally where Dr. V. Raymond Edman was the guest speaker. When he gave the altar call, I went forward with the assurance that God was leading me and that He would be with me in all things. Little did I know at that time what the "all things" would mean.

When Ernie asked me to marry him my decision had already been made and we began to make plans for the future. I gave my resignation to the Visiting Nurses' Association. Instead of accepting my resignation, they gave me six months' leave of absence. Although sure of the course I had chosen, I appreciated their gesture.

The summer of 1939 and the following year I attended Nyack Institute. Between summer work with the VNA and part-time work at the school, my financial needs were supplied.

Ernie had contacted the Mission board asking approval for our engagement. That meant that I was more or less on trial while attending Nyack.

Our plans took an abrupt turn when Ernie discovered that to keep his residence privileges in Netherlands East Indies he would have to be back within one year. I continued to work and we planned to be married.

On December 11, 1940, Ernie and I were married in the Kensington Alliance Church in Buffalo, New York.

War clouds were hanging very low. Europe was already engaged in World War II. I could not obtain an American passport to the Netherlands East Indies. The United States government refused to issue passports to American women for any overseas countries. Since I was married to a Canadian, however, and therefore enjoyed dual citizenship, we applied to the Canadian government. They granted me a passport. Once again, I could not have foreseen in that moment how significant that passport would prove to be in the days ahead.

We were on tour in Canada when word came from the New York Mission board that we must be ready to sail from the west coast on May 3, 1941. We had only one month to pack and say our farewells. I will never forget Ernie's last words to his mother and father: "If I do not see you on this earth again, 'I will see you in the morning, just inside the eastern gate.' "

Then it was time to say goodbye to my mother and father, eight brothers, two sisters-in-law, one niece, one nephew and my grandmother. I decided to trust, even as Paul the Apostle had, that I could do all things.

We sailed from San Francisco on May 3, 1941. At last we were really on our honeymoon.

During the voyage, God spoke to me through a verse from Esther 4:14: "And who knoweth whether thou art come to the kingdom for such a time as this?" Many times in the difficult years that were ahead, I asked myself (and the Lord), "For such a time as this?"

We finally reached Manila. While Ernie proceeded to Borneo by plane, I stayed in Manila. I had just missed a ship to Makassar, and besides, I did not yet have a visa for the Netherlands East Indies. Ernie had to leave, however, in order to make his resident deadline.

The day finally came when I said goodbye to my friends at the Baptist Mission Home in Manila who had given me such kind hospitality. Farewells were getting more frequent, but not any easier.

The trip through the many islands was beautiful. But, in fact, I felt very much alone. On July 25, 1941, the ship docked in Makassar. I strained my eyes looking for Ernie. I couldn't find him. My heart sank. *Surely he is here somewhere*, I thought to myself. He said he would be and Ernie was always a man of his word.

Finally, I recognized two missionaries by their picture. They smiled and waved excitedly.

"Where is Ernie?" I asked as soon as I had cleared customs.

"He hasn't come yet," was their response. No one

seemed to know when Ernie would arrive from the old station in Long Berang. But for me, it was not a pleasant turn of events.

The next day, however, we were at the wharf to meet him. As he walked toward me, joy welled up in my heart. This was the man I loved. But his appearance? His hair was much longer than usual. His clothes didn't fit him. His trousers were much too short. I had not seen him for over a month, but I certainly didn't expect this. *Was this the man I had married*? I wondered almost aloud.

The reason for the delay—and the strange appearance—we soon found out was that the canoe had upset in the rapids coming downstream from Long Berang. Ernie had borrowed another man's clothes—a Dutchman who was much shorter than Ernie's six-foot-one-inch frame.

With our first separation behind us, we tackled as best we could the important, urgent work before us. Rev. J.W. Brill, principal of the Makassar Bible School, was going home on furlough. Ernie was appointed to succeed him as head of the school.

My assignment was to learn the Malay language. I set about it diligently. With some delays, Ernie and I settled into our home. Delays of all kinds, I soon learned, were a familiar part of life in the island world.

I had been in Makassar only three days when I had my first attack of dengue fever, a gift from the hordes of mosquitos which invaded our home each evening.

Russell and Darlene Deibler lived a few blocks

down the street. When Darlene heard I was sick, she came to visit.

"Good morning," she greeted through the bedroom door. "So you have dengue fever?"

"Yes, it's a bad way to start my life in Makassar, isn't it?" I responded.

Like most missionaries, Darlene knew from experience what dengue fever was all about and could sympathize with my discomfort.

And ants! My mother had given me some powerful little ant cups. Every ant on the island must have known about those ant cups. They came by the droves. The only solution, I was advised, was to put kerosene cups under the legs of the food cupboard. That seemed to work.

The sounds of Makassar soon became familiar. The signal call to worship for the Mohammedans was a very prominent sound that gave me chills each time I heard it. But every Mohammedan would kneel down on his prayer rug and say, "There is one God and only one and Mohammed is his prophet." Their statement was a blanket denial of the deity of Christ, the One whom we were serving.

Other routine sounds made their way through both the light and darkness. People sold their wares up and down the streets. Dogs barked, roosters crowed, hens squawked. An occasional car passed by, loudly honking its rubber squeeze-horn. Sometimes the click-clack of a horse-drawn, two-wheeled buggy could be heard.

Then, five months into our ministry in Makassar, the alarming news came—Japan had bombed Pearl Harbor!

5

"Pigi!"

*"The angel of the LORD encampeth round
about them that fear him, and delivereth them."
(Psalm 34:7)*

Now in Benteng Tinggi, with the men gone, life had to go on. Each of us settled into our own little daily, constricted routines—tending the garden, reading, Bible study, prayer, walks within the boundaries of the property and fellowship with each other.

Trippi and Jackie, the Jaffray's two "sophisticated" mongrel dogs, helped to provide entertainment in the midst of a rather dismal situation. The first time Dr. Jaffray introduced the dogs to me, he explained, "Trippi is Presbyterian and Jackie is Christian and Missionary Alliance. They speak Malay."

Trippi was a dachshund type with short legs, turned-out toes and a short tail. He had long ears that twitched periodically. Trippi walked around very proudly, head held high, with a "I know exactly what I'm doing" air. But when spoken to, he only grunted.

Jackie, on the other hand, was taller and looked like a hunting dog with short, tan hair. Jackie always responded happily to human attention, wagging his long tail and looking up with friendly, understanding eyes.

After Ernie left, Jackie became my special friend. He seemed to know that something was wrong. I was now living in Lilian's house with the other single women—Margaret Kemp, Philoma Seeley and Lilian Marsh. (Darlene was staying with the Jaffrays.)

My room had an outside door that opened onto a garden. Every morning, without fail, Jackie opened my door and walked in and over to my desk where I was studying. He would lay in a patch of sunlight at my feet under the table. About an hour later, he would leave quietly and go about his business. Jackie had not done this before Ernie went away.

I was glad for the good books that were available at the Jaffrays. One book, in particular, impressed me—*The Splendor of God*, the story of Adoniram Judson, pioneer missionary to Burma.

About halfway through the book, I said to Ernie, "I don't think I should be reading this book right now."

"Why not?" he asked, surprised by the comment.

"Oh, I don't know. I have a strange feeling about it. The circumstances of the story are too much like what we are in. So far in the book, Adoniram and his wife had a three-year-old child die. Also the wife of another missionary dies. Finally, Mrs. Judson has to return to America because of poor health. They were separated for a whole year. Then, when she returned, Adoniram was taken prisoner and suffered under horrible conditions. I know these kinds of things can happen."

"Yes, my dear," Ernie responded sympathetically, "these kinds of things do sometimes happen."

Despite my apprehension, I continued to read the book. I put it away a second time. Then, finally, in the third session, I finished it. The powerful faith that shone through those pages proved to be a great inspiration in the trials that lay just ahead.

One day Margaret Jaffray sent for me. Darlene was very sick. I don't know what the medical diagnosis of her case would have been, but she was sick for several weeks. Every day I spent some time with her. Our fellowship was strengthened by the common sense of loss which weighed daily on our hearts and minds.

Sometimes at night we had uninvited visitors— thieves. We rigged up improvised alarms of tin cans and other noise makers. If a thief broke into any of the houses, the noise of the tin cans rang out over the hillside. We suspected that the "salesmen" who came around during the day offering their wares turned into thieves at night.

One day, when the Japanese made one of their unwelcome visits, they warned us that we were to have no contact with the nationals. They were not to visit us and we were not to visit them. It was a difficult situation, for almost daily there were people at our door.

Two Christian men appeared at my door with a proposition. They wanted to go to Malino and ask the authorities if I could have permission to help the nationals in time of sickness or trouble.

I assured them that that would be fine with me, but that they might get into trouble just by asking.

"We will try, Nonya (Mrs.)," they said.

That afternoon they returned to my door.

"Puji Tuhan (Praise the Lord)!" they said. "The officials gave you permission to help us."

With that, he handed me a piece of lined paper which had been folded three times. I opened it and read.

"Nonya Presswood has permission to help in time of sickness and trouble."

Just how much authority those words and signature would have carried before the secret police I did now know. Fortunately, such an occasion never arose and I was able to serve my national friends in many ways while we were at Benteng Tinggi.

In the early evenings, we would meet at the Jaffrays' for fellowship, Bible reading and prayer. There was always much to pray for and think about. What was happening to all the missionaries, including our husbands? Where were the Bible school students and workers? How were they managing to survive? When would our husbands be free again? When would we be free again? There were many questions, but the answers to them all were known only to God.

Dr. Jaffray was convinced that the Japanese would not win the war. He would quote from the 37th Psalm: "I have seen the wicked in great power, and spreading himself like a green bay tree. Yet he passed away. . ."

In those prayer meetings, I joined in prayer for

tribes and workers of other areas, some with strange, unfamiliar names. With Dr. Jaffray and Darlene, who had been in New Guinea, we prayed for the tribes that hadn't been reached: the Ekari, Danis, Uhundunis, Damals, Monis and others. (The stories of how the gospel reached these tribes are chronicled in *Cannibal Valley*, *"Weak Thing" in Moni Land*, *The People that Time Forgot*, and *God's Invasion*, all published by Christian Publications.)

A year had passed since we had received any letters or any reliable news from the outside world and it was now seven months since Russell and Ernie had been taken away. We had learned, however, that Ernie and Russell had been interned in Makassar in a police barracks with 150 civilian internees. Some of our Christian brethren were able to see them from time to time, but were not allowed to talk to them. The captured men, we were told, were forced to do menial tasks, even to pulling heavy wooden ox carts down the streets of Makassar like beasts of burden.

We sent a few notes, but it was a dangerous undertaking in that no communications of any kind were to pass in or out of Makassar.

One day, a national Christian arrived at our door. He had ridden all the way from Makassar to Benteng Tinggi—a distance of 70 kilometers—on his bicycle.

He handed me a pencil. I stared at it.

"It's from Tuan (Teacher) Presswood," he said.

It was my own pencil, the one I had given Ernie with the pen on one end and the pencil on the other. My first thought was that something had happened to Ernie. I tried the pencil. It worked. But the pen didn't.

Then I had a second thought.

Unscrewing the pen, I found a note written on rice paper and rolled up inside the rubber tubing of the pen.

"We are doing all right," it said. "Rice, sometimes fruit or vegetables to eat. Possibly men moving to Pare Pare 100 miles up the coast. Friends outside look at us with compassion. I love you, Ernie."

Russell and Ernie were alive!

Another time Ernie was able to send a can of peanut butter made from fresh peanuts. He knew how much I liked fresh peanut butter. Each little indication that Ernie was alive was like a ray of light from God Himself.

Sometime later, via the grapevine, I heard that Ernie was sick with severe dysentery. He was taken first to a hospital in the city and then was put on a Dutch hospital ship at sea along with 200 other English and American men. The Japanese had even allowed him to take his Bible! It was the only one on board the ship.

The Bible was passed from one man to another every 15 minutes from morning until night as long as there was light enough to read. Three men expressed their desire to accept Christ as their personal Savior. (That well-worn Bible, patched with shoe leather, is still in my possession.)

The Japanese continued to check on us from time to time. We felt like animals in the zoo because so many of them came to look us over.

Much of their time was spent just staring silently at us. It was unnerving. With their limited knowledge of the English language, each group asked us the same basic questions: Where are you from? How many are in this house? Have you been to Japan? What are you doing here?

We recognized some of the Japanese. They had worked in the stores in Makassar. Dr. Jaffray's barber turned out to be an officer in the Japanese Navy.

One curious man seemed to enjoy examining everything on our living room table. He, too, was curious looking in his own way, dressed in a short-sleeved uniform with shorts, his socks held up with navy blue men's garters—the kind that hooked onto the socks. He had probably gotten them from some white man's trunk—perhaps Ernie's.

After the curious soldier and I passed some time of silence together—he staring at our table and me staring at his unique outfit—he turned to me and said in broken English, "You go Japan?"

Fear stabbed my heart. We had heard rumors that the Japanese were going to take the white women to Japan. We had also heard what the soldiers had done to the women in Malino only two miles away. I was terrified.

Finally, I blurted out, "Now?"

He looked at me rather perturbed and said, "No! No!"

I was relieved and finally figured out that what he really wanted to know was whether I had ever been to Japan!

Another soldier, as he was going out the door,

said to me, "You hate Roosevelt!" We all found this comment quite amusing because in our political discussions among ourselves, I was the only one who sided with President Roosevelt! As a public health nurse, I had remembered how his many projects had provided work for poverty-stricken people during the Depression.

Another day, during the dry season, we spotted a forest fire down in the valley. It appeared so far away that we felt sure it wouldn't come to our compound. But the fire crept closer and closer.

We consoled ourselves that the paved road about 20 feet below our homes would stop the fire. It didn't. The flames leaped the road to the dry weeds on our side. Nationals and missionaries alike ran for anything in which to fetch water from the trickling spring. We dumped water on the parched ground making a wide half circle trying to prevent the fire from reaching any structure.

Just as the flames reached Lilian's house, the breeze reversed itself back over the burned-off area. We realized later how absurd it had been for so few of us to even think that we could put out a forest fire with so little water. But God knew our limited resources. He had changed the wind in our favor. He had put the fire out for us.

In October 1942, seven months after Russell and Ernie had been taken, we heard that they had been moved from the Makassar police barracks to Pare Pare, a town about 100 miles up the western coast. Other rumors—that we were going to be moved somewhere, that white women were being taken to Japan, that the Japanese were still enjoying military victories—only added to our restlessness and fear.

On December 29, 1942, the Japanese paid us a visit that would forever change the course of our lives. We were ordered to prepare for evacuation. We could take only what we could carry ourselves. They also confiscated what little money we had left after living for a year without any income.

Each of us packed a suitcase. Then we filled a couple of wash tubs with pails, pans, blankets, mosquito nets and other items we felt we might need.

A Japanese soldier watched me as I packed.

Finally, he said, "Ambil banyak apa apa. Banyak susah datang!" (Take many things. Much trouble is coming!) He evidently knew something that we did not, could not, know.

When our suitcases and other baggage had been loaded onto the truck, I set a lacquered Japanese box filled with needles, thread, etc., on top of my suitcase. While we were waiting for the next order to be given, the box disappeared. I finally spied it on the seat beside the truck driver and grabbed it.

The driver said, "Tidak, saya mau! (No, I want.)"

I answered boldly in Malay, "It's mine. I want." Neither I nor the driver knew in that moment how important those sewing materials would later prove to be. But my Heavenly Father knew.

With everything loaded on the truck, we were on our way. To where, we didn't know. At the end of the Mission driveway we turned left onto the main road. Now we knew at least one thing—our destination was not Makassar.

Malino. In normal times, Malino was a vacation

spot for the Dutch. I had been there a few times, including the visit to the Dutch doctor for the wart on my foot. The scenery was breathtaking—palm trees, flowering shrubs, cannas and other beautiful flora.

But, with the war, all had changed.

Our truck pulled into the open market area in late afternoon and parked behind another truck piled high with baggage. No one moved on the truck. We had learned not to speak until spoken to, not to move until ordered to. But when we heard "pigi lekas" (go fast), we knew there was no alternative.

One officer spoke to Darlene. Although I could understand none of it, it seemed like a friendly conversation. Afterwards, I asked Darlene what the officer had said.

She responded, "He told me that he had seen my husband and that he is doing fine. But," she added, "I don't trust him."

The time came to "pigi."

"Follow the path across the valley to the small house," the commanding officer instructed. "They," he said, (pointing to the coolies standing nearby), "will carry your luggage."

The coolies were all Bugis, a tribe from the Celebes Island. Their name alone struck fear to many hearts because of their reputation of being a treacherous people. But we had no choice and were thankful for anyone who would carry our bags.

The first group—the Jaffrays, Margaret Kemp, Lilian Marsh and Philoma Seely—marched off with Dr. Jaffray in the lead, each carrying his or her bag of personal items.

As Darlene described it in her book, *Evidence Not Seen*:

> *If it hadn't been so frightening, it would have been hilarious. Dr. Jaffray led the entourage, carrying his black satchel of "eau de cologne-medicines" in his left hand, his cane in his right. Mrs. Jaffray followed, wearing a black velvet cape lined in white satin—for which she thanked the Lord every time she put it on. She looked regal with her beautiful white hair as she stepped onto the path bearing in her arms a magnificent, large, silver soup tureen, formerly owned by Dr. Jaffray's favorite aunt. Then in single file the others followed after, Miss Seely bringing up the rear.*
>
> *Ruth and I, as the youngest, volunteered to follow with the carriers and the rest of the baggage. I wasn't about to let those Bugis men know how scared I was. We checked their loads, lined them up in single file, then ordered them to move out with Ruth at the head of the column and me positioned at the rear. I had agreed with Ruth that as soon as we hit the jungle, where it would be fairly dark, we would start circling them.*
>
> *I gave Ruth a signal, then counting in my most martial tones—Satu! Dua! Tiga! Empat!—I marched to the front of the line with Ruth circling to the rear doing the same thing.*
>
> *Reaching the first man in line, I shouted, 'Delapan belas! Eighteen!' As soon as I heard Ruth yell eighteen I'd retreat down the other*

*side, counting the men off again, and Ruth
would advance toward the front. We continued
this until we finally emerged from the jungle on
the other side of the valley. Reaching the small
house indicated by the officer we found the
others waiting for us.*

6

Kampili

"They that feared the LORD spake often one to another: and the LORD hearkened, and heard it, and a book of remembrance was written before him for them that feared the LORD, and that thought upon his name."
(Malachi 3:16)

It was now May 1943, 14 months since Ernie and Russell had been taken away and four months since we had moved to the little house down the jungle trail in Lambasang.

On May 2nd, another order was issued by the Japanese. All women and children were to be moved out of Lambasang and Malino. Once again questions flooded our minds: Where would we be taken next? What would our accommodations be like? When would the war be over? When would we be free?

There were many new rumors abroad. One was that we would be sent to a labor camp where we would "learn to work." The Japanese considered white women lazy, used to living in the lap of luxury.

Now, again, we had marching orders. Suitcases packed and tubs filled with utensils, we hiked our way over the now familiar (once a week we had walked this trail to collect our food rations) trail to Malino for the last time.

As we reached the village, we found a crowd of women and children wandering about aimlessly. Everyone seemed to be waiting for something to happen. Time for that "something," however, was running out, for it was getting dark. Finally, the order came that we were all to sleep in the already packed-to-the-doors Catholic church.

People shoved in and slept anywhere they could—on the tile floor or the narrow pews. The Dutch Catholic sisters who had been evacuated from Makassar chose the altar area.

The Jaffrays settled on the uncomfortable pews and the rest of us found a place nearby. We did not want to get separated from one another. I tried sleeping first on the bench, and then on the tile floor. Both were most uncomfortable, but at least it was dry. There was always something to be thankful for if one looked hard enough.

That night we all slept in our clothes. It was becoming a habit.

Daylight came and I was awakened by Darlene.

"Ruth," she whispered, "we need to make the trip to the washrooms before the crowd starts."

Dr. Jaffray, always an early riser, was up and ready for the day. Soon the other ladies awoke and we took turns watching the baggage. Breakfast was a piece of bread.

Then began the predictable wait for orders. About

a dozen Army trucks were eventually lined up and loaded with our baggage. Finally, we were told to climb into one that had hardly enough room for one, let alone eight more people. Before the trucks left, we were provided a demonstration that no doubt was orchestrated to humiliate and pacify us all.

The former mayor's wife from Makassar was knocked to the ground by one of the Japanese.

"Why was she knocked down?" someone nearby demanded.

Another voice asked, "What did she do?"

Still another, "Be quiet!"

That was good advice, for we didn't know who could be next and the Japanese weren't about to give a reason for anything they did.

Then, suddenly, with a jerk, the truck took off with Lilian, Margaret, Margaret Jaffray, Philoma, Darlene and me trying to balance ourselves on top of the baggage. (Dr. and Mrs. Jaffray rode in the cab of the truck.) We hung on to each other for dear life as the vehicle sped down the mountain road with all its twists and turns. Were we really out of control? Was the driver trying to ditch us or scare us to death? Either way, it was a very frightening ride. We were thankful when we finally reached level land.

This convoy of trucks contained all white women and children, the nationals who had married white spouses and those who had been found collaborating with the Americans. We were heading in the direction of Makassar.

As we passed through towns and villages, men, women and children lined up along the road waving Nippon flags or displaying the "thumbs up" sign as they shouted, "Orang Nippon." Their support for the Japanese, we decided, was probably an effort to save their own necks.

Two hours later we came to a place completely fenced in with barbed wire. We passed through a wide gate and bounced over a moat. As the truck turned into the gate, Darlene exclaimed, "So this is it—Kampili."

"Kampili? That doesn't mean anything to me. I have never heard of the place," I remarked.

"It used to be the national tuberculosis sanitarium," she replied.

Margaret Kemp chimed in. "We had a couple students from the Bible School here at one time."

Kampili Camp.

The truck lurched to a stop and the driver waved us off the truck. Groans filled the air as legs stiff from half-standing, half-sitting for two hours were forced into new positions. Hands and arms paralyzed by two hours of gripping whatever was nearby screamed for mercy. We were exhausted.

My eyes scanned the three-foot-high grass surrounding row upon row of long bamboo buildings. There were no trees to be seen inside the fences.

"These buildings look like places to keep animals," I remarked, turning to Lilian. "Perhaps we will have to take care of them."

"Maybe," Lilian answered.

As other trucks drove in and unloaded our group was herded to one of the block-long sheds.

"Do you think these are the houses we are going to live in?" I asked Philoma.

"It certainly looks like it," she answered cautiously.

Baggage in hand, I climbed up a ladder to the top bunk second from the shed door.

"This is great, Philoma," I said. "I always wondered what it would be like to sleep on the top bunk." How could I know that for more days than I wished to even think about that top bunk would be the only spot I had any claim to, the only refuge to commune with my own soul and with my Heavenly Father?

The sheds, or *loads* as the Dutch called them, had palm leaf roofs, dirt floors, woven bamboo walls and a row of bamboo bunk beds on either side of the aisle down the center of the building. The entire structure was tied together with rattan using no nails. Each shed accommodated 100 people.

To the extreme right of the camp gate was an area called the Ambon section—the original buildings of the sanitarium that boasted cement walls and tile floors. These sheds were now being occupied by people from Ambon Island, another target of the Japanese. Dr. Jaffray was assigned a room there with other men and boys over 16 years of age.

Although the Japanese were very good at organization, the process of assigning the sheds took considerable time. Any woman who acted boldly, by their judgment, was put in her place fast by being hit or knocked to the ground.

Most of our missionary group was assigned to Shed 8. Margaret Jaffray and her mother were assigned to another shed.

Shed 8 was special because it contained mostly

foreigners. What a mixture we were—Jews, Armenians, Czechoslovakians, Chinese, Irish, Scotch, Dutch, Germans, Australians, Canadians and Americans. Some were Christians and some were not.

We had been in the camp only a few days when we were introduced to the Japanese commander of Kampili Camp—Mr. Yamaji. He had transferred from the men's camp.

Yamaji was a short, fat man with piercing eyes. He lost no time in letting us know he ruled with cruel authority. We soon learned that he had a violent temper which was often unleashed with brutal force.

Yamaji appointed Mrs. Joustra, a Dutch woman, to oversee the 1,600 women and children in Kampili Camp. In time, other leaders were appointed over departments such as the kitchen, gardens, pig sty, hospital, sewing room and storage place.

In addition, two women doctors, Dr. Goedbloed and Dr. Fenster, and one man, Dr. Marseille, all of them prisoners, served the people of the camp with honor even though they had very limited supplies and equipment. However, they always had epsom salts! That seemed to be the only medication available.

The Japanese allowed us one Catholic priest, Father Bell, and one Protestant missionary, Rev. Spreeuwenberg, a Dutch missionary from New Guinea, as our spiritual leaders. These men were also prisoners of war. In addition to his pastorly duties, Rev. Spreeuwenberg did assorted menial tasks required by our overseers.

Darlene was chosen as our shed leader. It was her responsibility to carry out the orders of the Japanese and Mrs. Joustra, as well as to supervise the 100 assorted people who occupied Load 8. It was not an easy job, but her courage, charisma and trust in the Lord enabled her to carry it out capably. A great asset was her ability to communicate fluently in Malay, Dutch and English.

We had not had any word from Ernie and Russell in a long time. We knew they were in Pare Pare and we had heard that the men were treated more cruelly than the women.

It was announced at Kampili that all males over 15 years of age would be taken to Pare Pare and be interned there. Dr. Jaffray received the same order.

June 1, 1943, our group went over to the Ambon section to say goodbye. Dr. Jaffray appeared cheerful and quiet and committed us all to the Lord in prayer. He seemed to anticipate being with Russell and Ernie.

Before he left he gave me a *Hymns of the Christian Life* hymnal because I did not have one of my own.

Margaret Jaffray was very devoted to her father and had taken care of him in every possible way. Dr. Jaffray would miss the care and attention that Margaret gave him, but Margaret would also find a great void in her life.

I gave a handkerchief to Dr. Jaffray, asking him to take it to Ernie. It was an old one with a special embroidered message in one corner—a U-shaped island. I knew that Ernie would understand that I was saying, "I love you."

It was sad for all of us when Dr. Jaffray left. The

last year had taken a great toll on him. Now, at age 70, he was being separated from the two people he loved most—his wife and daughter.

The Japanese made the rounds every night for roll call. We stood at attention at the foot of our beds. The first time they came through, a Dutchman led the way. With every step, he said, "Achter me komt de Commandant; dames baughen!"

That was my first lesson in Dutch! I learned rather quickly that it meant, "After me comes the commander; women bow!"

The ritual became a custom after that. When the camp bell rang at 7 p.m., Darlene and the leaders of each shed stood at the front door of their respective sheds until the commander came. Sometimes he would only salute the leader at the door and go on his way and sometimes he would stride through the shed. We never knew what to expect.

We had instructions to bow every time we met a Japanese. The higher the rank, the lower we were to bow. It was always difficult for me to know whether I had bowed low enough or not.

It was strenuous work just to maintain life. The schedules of the work crews changed from time to time, but some things we all had to do—cooking, carrying water and wood, washing clothes and the like. We were truly "hewers of wood and drawers of water."

The water was pulled up from wells by a rope with a pail. Often the rope broke and the pail fell to the bottom. The wells had to be deepened more than once. The well used by Shed 8 was covered with a bamboo shack. This provided us a place to bathe. We were grateful.

The second well, with a diameter of about 12 feet, stood open with a stone wall around it. It reminded me of pictures I had seen of biblical wells. I liked going to that well for it seemed that an Unseen Guest was present there. How I needed the water that He could provide!

Our day started at 7 a.m. There was always an assignment before breakfast—calisthenics, gathering *kankung* (a spinach-like vegetable) from the irrigated fields with water up to our hips, or chopping *alang alang* (a three-foot-high grass) with a big hoe. Whatever the job, we had done a day's work before the regular day's work began. The Japanese were truly carrying out their threat. We white women were learning what hard labor was!

The staple food was rice. It came in 100-pound sacks which had to be carried by us women from the trucks to the cooking areas. Then it had to be pounded, winnowed and cooked before we could eat it. Fortunately, there were people in the camp who knew how to do these things. The rest of us soon learned.

Rice was on the menu for every meal—rice porridge for breakfast, boiled rice for lunch and boiled rice for dinner. Sometimes the rice was very good, sometimes very poor.

For meat, we had water buffalo. Every part of it! It was cut up into small pieces and served in salty broth. Rumors were that at times we were eating other kinds of meat, too. Fortunately we did not know what we were eating nor when.

Another specialty was *sajur licin* or slippery vegetable as we called it. It truly was slimy stuff. We also ate the tops of sweet potatoes. When we could get it, small amounts of *sambal* (sauce made with tiny red peppers) made the rice a little more palatable.

All drinking water had to be boiled in huge oil drums which sat on three piles of bricks with the fire built underneath. Wood for the fire had to be carried from the go-down (shed). Sometimes it was dry and sometimes it was wet and very green. Carrying wood was one of my first assignments. I suppose I looked young and strong. (In our group in 1943, Darlene at 27 was the youngest. I was 33 and Margaret Jaffray was near my age. Lilian, Margaret and Philoma were in their 40s and Dr. and Mrs. Jaffray, 70 and 72 respectively.)

It was Darlene's job to assign the jobs which had been handed down from the top through Mrs. Joustra. She approached me.

"Ruth," she said, "in light of the fact that you grew up with so many brothers, would you mind being in charge of the 13 boys who live in our shed? Your job will be carrying wood and other articles from the go-down to the kitchen."

The loads of sticks tied together with rattan, I soon found out, were very heavy and I felt guilty having the young boys carry such heavy loads. But the truth was that all of us were working far beyond the limit of our strength.

Another of my jobs was the appointed position of nurse for Shed 8. It seemed, however, that I was rarely present when Dr. Marseille made his rounds—I was either off on some other job or sick in the hospital myself. Also, I did not understand Dutch, so the position was short-lived.

We were becoming accustomed to all kinds of back-breaking work—digging ditches for air raid shelters, cleaning cesspools, hauling dirt and water. And all the while there was the burning tropical sun.

7

Camp Life in Kampili

*"In all these things we are more than conquerors
through him that loved us."
(Romans 8:37)*

The place I called home—the second upper
bed on the left from the front door of Shed
8—was in a good neighborhood. Darlene had
the first upper bunk and Margaret Kemp the lower.
Philoma occupied the bunk under me.

The next five bunks on the other side of me were
occupied by a missionary from Holland, Mrs. Van
de Haarst, and her four teenage daughters—Leinie,
Tina, Mien and Katrina. Across the way, along the
right side of the shed, Lilian had the top bunk and
Mrs. Woodward, a Salvation Army missionary from
Scotland, the lower bunk. The two bunks beside
them were occupied by Mrs. Snaith and her
daughter, Emerald, about 10 years old. They were
from Ireland and were also with the Salvation Army.

Then came Maus Dol, her daughter, Paxja, and
her mother, Mrs. Zimmerman. Next to them were
Mrs. Verschoor and her daughter, Anneka. We
made up the first block of Shed 8.

When we first arrived, the thing we wanted most was privacy. We put up some discarded sheets for curtains, but when the Japanese made their rounds, they ordered all curtains taken down. The same thing happened with our *tempat mandi*, the bath place. The bamboo enclosure had a well in the center. To take a bath, we had to draw the water up from the well with a pail and then pour the water into another container. After scrubbing clean with laundry soap, we used a dipper or tin can to rinse off the soap. This dipper bath was very refreshing and worked fine as long as there was plenty of water.

During the dry season—two to three months out of every year—water was scarce and we had to use muddy water for bathing and washing clothes. Water of any kind was preserved and, in its final form, used to wash down the toilets.

We all slept under mosquito nets. Although their protection was mostly only a perception, I did feel safe when I was under my net. The net hung from the rafters at four corners and tucked under the *tikar* (reed mat) which served as the mattress. A blanket was needed all year as the nights had a damp, penetrating chill.

Rats were plentiful. They loved to squeal and run back and forth on the bamboo rafters overhead. They rarely bothered us as long as we didn't bother them, although at times it seemed like they owned the place.

One night, I was awakened out of a sound sleep by someone or something pulling my hair. In the darkness, I was unable to discover anything amiss.

The next morning, however, my head was bleeding and the mosquito net beside my head had two holes in it, one about the size of a grapefruit and the other the size of an orange. The rats had evidently come visiting. After that, I slept with my suitcase inside the net to protect my head.

The toilets were at the rear of the sheds and separate from them. They consisted of cement floors with open holes over cesspools. That was it. Our visits there were no longer than absolutely necessary, believe me. We tried to keep them reasonably clean, but even a cursory inspection would explain why so much dysentery plagued the camp.

From time to time, the cesspools had to be emptied. Cleaning the cesspools was one of those extra jobs on top of what we were already assigned. A tin can was used as a dipper to plunge down into the hole and lift out the putrifying contents complete with maggots and many unmentionable etceteras. We then dumped the can into a *blik* (20 gallon oil tin). The *blik* had a rattan handle which was slipped onto a bamboo pole and then carried by two women, one on either end, to a dirt hole the size of a large swimming pool.

Darlene and I had our turns at this distasteful job. We stood precariously at the edge of the "swimming pool" and dumped the barrel.

"Don't get too near the edge," Darlene would warn. I didn't even want to think about it.

Mrs. Snaith, one of my neighbors in the shed, did have the misfortune to fall in. She had gotten too close to the soft edge. We all felt so sorry for her and helped give her a thorough scrub-down. Poor soul! She kept wanting to bathe again and again. Someone found some iodine, an unheard of item in the camp, and placed it on her athlete's foot lesions.

The hospital was situated in the center of the camp beyond the commander's office. These were the original cement buildings connected with the former tuberculosis sanitarium. Before the war, both the Catholics and the Salvation Army had operated hospitals in Makassar. The nurses who now supervised the camp hospital were Catholic nuns and Salvation Army nurses from these two hospitals. Unfortunately, I ended up in the hospital on three different occasions because of acute illnesses.

Mrs. Snaith, the Irish lady from Shed 8, and I became special friends on my first trip to the hospital. We both had dysentery and our beds were next to one another. Her husband, Major Snaith, a Salvation Army officer, was interned with our men in Pare Pare. Mrs. Snaith loved the Lord and lived her faith without compromise. She also had a refreshing Irish wit. When she slapped her thigh or said, "Oh jolly," I always knew that something humorous was coming.

With the second attack of dysentery, I became extremely weak. The whole camp was affected. About 500 (half of the camp) were down at one time. Doctors Goedbloed and Fenster had only enough dysentery medication in injection form for three people. They gave one injection to a doctor's wife, one to the child of a doctor in Pare Pare and one to me. The doctor's wife and baby died. Many others died as well.

My third trip to the hospital was brought on by a chest condition. I had the strange feeling that I was going to die and, what's more, the scriptures I read seemed to confirm this. I had borrowed a devotional book by Spurgeon and on that particular date his subject was death and dying.

The doctors diagnosed my case as bronchitis and ordered cold wet sheets wrapped around my chest to relieve the congestion and reduce the fever. The next day I was much worse, probably with pneumonia. I was coughing and spitting up blood.

One afternoon, Philoma Seely came to see me. I told her that I felt my death was imminent and that the scriptures seemed to confirm it. Before leaving, she prayed with me and promised to continue to make my condition a definite matter of prayer.

The following afternoon, as she walked through the doorway, her face was beaming.

"Ruth," she said, "I spent most of the night in prayer until the early morning hours. Then the answer came. You are not going to die! You are going to live and declare the works of the Lord!"

I believed her, and from that time on I began to get well.

One day it was my duty to help cook the rice for 100 people. I had been out gathering sticks, twigs, grass—anything to help get the wet, green wood to burn. Many others had been doing the same thing. All the grounds had been picked clean. As we began to prepare the rice, an emergency alarm was sounded by Mr. Yamaji. It was the signal for an approaching tornado. Everyone was to take shelter in the sheds.

I could see the black clouds heading toward us as I ran across the gangway from the kitchen to the shed. The rain began to come in torrents propelled by the fierce winds. We crouched inside the pitch-dark shed with all the windows and doors shut, holding our breath as the wind roared and the bamboo cracked around us.

When the all clear sign came, we rushed outside to see what damage had been done.

The tornado had picked up the kitchen from its cement base and flattened it. Then the funnel had made a U-turn, destroying the storage shed where the rice and other foods and materials were kept. It finally careened off across the countryside. Thankfully, no one was hurt. God had provided a shelter in the time of storm.

The sun began to break through the clouds, beaming its rays through the last few raindrops. What a sight to behold—two beautiful rainbows shining over the camp! To me, they were a sign of hope, hope of God's love and mercy. Not one of the occupied sheds had been destroyed.

We certainly had plenty of scattered bamboo to burn for months to come. Our picked clean yard had become a landscape of twisted and broken sticks in a matter of a few minutes. But the tornado was actually a blessing in disguise, because bamboo burns much better than wood and makes a very hot fire. It would be so much easier to bring the water to a boil in those large drums.

Excitement of another kind erupted another day.

A ship that had been bombed was towed into Makassar harbor. Old clothes from the ship, many of them made of denim, were brought to the camp sewing room. The seams of the blue jeans were loaded with bed bugs, an additional "gift" which we had to squash! Fortunately, they had not bitten anyone in a long time and were quite sluggish.

In addition, bolts and bolts of water-soaked material were dumped on the ground. Our job was to unroll the cloth and spread it on the ground to dry. It was then carried to the sewing room to be made into uniforms for the women and children.

The uniform was a short romper-type outfit, buttoned down the front. At the time, Margaret Kemp and I were working in the sewing room with about 50 other women. The sewing machines were really humming. Besides making these uniforms, we also made clothes for the Japanese—shirts, undergarments and caps. Japanese guards would inspect us and our work as they walked up and down the rows of sewing machines.

Once, while I was working on one of the caps that had two black bands for trim, two officers stopped behind me. I could feel their stares. They exchanged some words in Japanese. I knew that those black bands had to be sewed precisely to predetermined measurements. *Was I doing it right?* I wondered to myself. If they weren't done right, we were forced to rip them out and do them over again. I was also fearful because only a few days before Margaret and Philoma had been hauled off by the *kempetei*. Could it be that my turn was coming?

I was relieved when the officers moved on.

Straight pins were very scarce. I had only seven pins to work with and some of those were bent. But they were precious. They helped me through many a sewing job, especially those that involved the black bands.

Once in a while, when a piece of material was left over, the Japanese allowed one of the women to keep it for herself. One day my turn came to receive a piece of khaki cloth large enough to make a skirt to wear over my rompers.

Those days working in the sewing room proved a great blessing to me, a much-needed and welcome respite from the hard labor of other tasks. Although I didn't know it at the time, my strength was being preserved for the dark days that still lay ahead.

8

Bad News on All Fronts

"From the end of the earth will I cry unto thee,
when my heart is overwhelmed: lead me to the
rock that is higher than I."
(Psalm 61:2)

Russell and Ernie in Pare Pare were allowed to write 40-word notes to Darlene and me from time to time. The notes were always censored and typewritten on military forms. I received four such letters from Ernie while I was in Kampili Camp.

Often with the letters came a pair of *klombs* (wooden shoes) which the men had made in Pare Pare. The arrival of the letters and *klombs* were at the least a sign that our husbands were still alive and we were always overjoyed to receive them.

In the fall of 1943, some wooden shoes were delivered to the camp. Darlene received a pair from Russell, but there was something wrong—the *klombs* were unfinished.

I examined my pair of *klombs*, searching for some

kind of message from Ernie. Under one strap I finally found a message scrawled very lightly: "Russell died."

I was shocked. I didn't know what to do. How could I keep such news from Darlene? And I certainly did not dare to tell anyone else, because the Japanese would surely find out that messages were being relayed in other than the approved channels and the couriers would be in trouble. Both the men's camps and the women's camps would suffer severe consequences, to say nothing of the repercussions to each missionary personally.

The day came when I could no longer keep the news to myself. I decided to confide in Lilian, the senior missionary of our group. Lilian's response was, "Do not breathe this to anyone. It must not be known through us." I took her warning to heart.

Days went by and then weeks. I prayed earnestly that the officials would soon break the news to Darlene.

Finally, about three months later (Russell died on August 28, 1943), Mrs. Joustra, our camp leader, came to Shed 8. She approached Darlene, spoke with her briefly and then she and Darlene walked out of the barracks to a spot were they could be alone. I knew in my heart why Mrs. Joustra wanted to talk alone with Darlene. I was so thankful that this kind, understanding Dutch lady had been chosen to break the tragic news.

That night, after dark, Darlene and I walked the grounds around the shed with our arms around one another. I can still see Darlene, dressed in her navy blue pajamas, silent, and with a strained expression on her face.

"Lord," I cried, "what can I say? What can I do to help?"

The only verse that came to mind was Second Corinthians 1:4: "[He] comforteth us in all our tribulation, that we may be able to comfort them which are in any trouble, by the comfort wherewith we ourselves are comforted of God."

I certainly did not have a neat package of comfort to hand to Darlene. I had not experienced such pain. I had never lost a husband, or for that matter, anyone close in my family. Her hurt was too deep, the question "why" too fresh. Darlene and Russell had loved each other deeply. Only God through His Holy Spirit could comfort and bring her through.

Darlene, as always, exhibited a brave and courageous exterior. But from that day on there was a change in her. Someone very precious had been taken from her life. A part of her seemed to have died.

By the end of 1943, things became considerably more difficult in the camp. Food was scarce, though sometimes we feasted when the Japanese celebrated some special observance day. We had to work harder. Almost everyone in the camp was sick with dysentery, malaria, hepatitis, beri beri or tropical ulcers. But all of us had to keep going as we were usually responsible for not one job, but several. If we went to get help from the clinic, the answer was always epsom salts. It was the only medicine now available.

Many more Japanese were coming to the camp as visitors. During the dry season we had to sprinkle the roads so they wouldn't get their boots dusty. The visitors scrutinized everything. The higher the rank of the officer, the lower we had to bow. Bowing became so automatic for us that the habit later proved difficult to break.

From all appearances, the internees were conscientiously obeying the rules, but the Japanese didn't see it that way. All kinds of punishments were inflicted for supposed infractions. Some women were beaten. Others were forced to stand in the sun for hours at a time.

Another favorite punishment of the commanders was to send the women out to catch flies. How we caught the flies didn't seem to matter as long as we brought in 100, 200, 300 depending on how "bad" the commander thought we had been. To get it over with in the shortest possible time, we went to the pig sty. There were always thousands of flies near the pig sty!

Hundreds of pigs were raised in our camp in quarters that were better than our own. Their floors were scrubbed cement. Ours were dirt. The pigs were treated like pets. Even the women who cared for the pigs received special attention from the Japanese.

One day, the commander asked for more volunteers to take care of the pigs. No one volunteered.

"All right," he said. "If there are no volunteers, I will choose some."

So, on a scorching hot day, the commander summoned the women from all 16 sheds to report outside his office. The occupants of each shed were lined up in single file. I had just gotten out of the hospital with the chest condition and felt very weak from the ordeal. Standing in the hot sun didn't help.

As we stood at attention, the commander went up and down the rows, singling out the women he wanted. As he came closer and closer to me, I felt the fearful certainty that I would be chosen.

Sure enough, he pulled me out of the line and then proceeded down the rows choosing still others.

Wild thoughts raced through my head. *Me? Feeding, bathing and scrubbing pigs? Delivering piglets? Keeping pig pens clean?* Though I had grown up on a farm, I was supposed to be "feminine." I had never had anything to do with pigs. And worse than what the pigs would demand was the fear of what the Japanese men might demand in the way of special favors from the women who took care of the pigs. I shuddered at the thought.

When the commander's quota was met, we were dismissed. We heard nothing more for 24 hours. I prayed continually and I knew Margaret and Lilian were praying for me as well as others. Darlene spoke to Yamaji on my behalf, explaining that because of my weakened condition I would find the task very difficult. Yamaji responded, "All right. But you must find a substitute for her."

At last, word came that some woman had "volunteered." I would not have to report to the pig sty.

9

Enemies–Human and Otherwise

"Through God we shall do valiantly:
for he it is that shall tread down our enemies."
(Psalm 60:12)

One day in April 1944, a big black *kempeitai* (secret police/shock troops) limousine entered the gate and drove up the lane to the camp. Obviously its occupants were high-ranking officers. The vehicle stopped at the commander's headquarters. We knew that trouble was ahead.

The Japanese officers, it was rumored, were searching for American spies and especially for hidden radios or other means of communication. Shortly after the limousine arrived, Margaret Kemp, who worked in the sewing room, was summoned to the office. A few minutes later the commander's assistant headed for the garden to summon Philoma Seely to the office.

After about 15 minutes, which seemed more like an hour, both women were ushered to the limousine, along with a number of others with Dutch connections.

As the limousine headed toward the gate, about 50 of us ran along the roadside to wave and say goodbye. We wanted the women to know that we cared about them and that we would be standing with them in prayer. They did not wave back.

As soon as the limousine was out the gate, Yamaji bellowed angrily, "What's wrong with you people? Are you glad to see them go? You are dumb!"

Of course, he misunderstood our actions, but he knew plenty that we did not know. The routine explanation was that they were taken away to be examined.

The *kempeitai* operated on the order of the German gestapo. Surely in the natural there was much to fear, but the promises of God sustained us: "What time I am afraid, I will trust in thee" (Psalm 56:3), and "God hath not given us the spirit of fear; but of power, and of love, and of a sound mind" (2 Timothy 1:7).

This had not been the first time that the *kempeitai* limousine had driven into Kampili. Many women had been taken to Makassar before. Many never came back and those who did lived in silence.

What would happen to Margaret and Philoma?

We resumed our work, work which became a blessing as it enabled us to carry the emotional burden that was on us. It was difficult to be light-hearted. The women in Shed 8 gathered together when we could to sing and pray and just to talk with one another.

May 10th was Darlene's 27th birthday and a surprise party was planned. There was a cake—a very solid cake made with rice flour—which even boasted frosting made from raw sugar and black coffee whipped together. The group pooled their coffee allotments so that coffee could be served with the cake. Ingenious gifts of all kinds were made by the internees and presented to Darlene.

Two days after the big party, the *kempeitai* limousine once again pulled into Kampili and parked in front of the commander's headquarters.

Were they bringing Margaret and Philoma back? we wondered. We waited and we hoped. But the answer was no. They had brought no one back. Instead, Darlene was summoned.

"I knew in my heart that those men had come for me," Darlene wrote later. "I stood frozen, watching; then, as though drawn by a magnet, I started to walk toward the office. My dreaded premonition was confirmed; I was summoned to Yamaji's office."

"Dear Darlene! Why were they calling for her?"

"What ordeal must she go through?"

"Is it because she is American?"

These and other questions were being voiced all around me.

Mrs. Snaith said, "I'm so sorry. What can we do?"

Everyone in our shed was stunned because Darlene, as our leader, was dear to each one. Not much was said, but much was felt. On the outside we had become stoic and seemingly helpless. But many of us were conscious that we still had access to the throne of God through Jesus Christ and were certain that there was power in prayer and in that Name.

Days passed with more sickness. Dysentery was rampant. The toll rose from 400 to 500 people stricken. Air raids came more often, too. Trouble in many guises came almost daily.

Now, only a few of our group were left: Mrs. Jaffray and Margaret, who were Canadian. They still were quartered in the Ambon section of the camp and, as far as I know, knew nothing of the episode with Margaret and Philoma or of Darlene's disappearance from the camp.

In Shed 8 only Lilian Marsh, who was from England, and I, with my dual Canadian-U.S. citizenship, were left. We were in terrible suspense, wondering who would be taken next.

One day, Commander Yamaji came to our barracks to pay Lilian and me a visit. He was smiling as he came through the door. That helped to put us slightly more at ease. He said that he had taken Darlene some bananas and a mosquito net.

Then Yamaji turned to me: "Berapa saudara laki-laki nonya ada?" (How many brothers do you have?)

I replied, "Delapan" (eight).

His reply was, "Bukan main; itu terlalu banyak!" (There is no kidding about that; that is too many!)

Actually, Yamaji probably already knew the answer to his own questions because the Japanese knew all about us. We had reason to believe the walls had ears in those days. We hardly dared talk to one another.

Then, a few days later, I was summoned to the

office. My legs suddenly became limp as I headed
off toward the commander's headquarters. The
walk seemed very long. Indeed, it was long enough
for a passage from Luke 12 to come to mind: "And
when they bring you unto the synagogues, and
unto magistrates, and powers, take ye no thought
how or what thing ye shall answer, or what ye shall
say. For the Holy Ghost shall teach you in the
same hour what ye ought to say."

I stepped through the door. Several Japanese
were standing there, apparently waiting for my arrival. I made my low bows, hoping once again that
they were low enough.

One officer asked, "What is your name?"

"Ruth Presswood."

"Are you Canadian?"

"Yes, Tuan," I answered quietly. I was thankful
that they didn't press the issue, because I was born
American but now had dual citizenship because of
my marriage to a Canadian.

An officer took a number off the board on the
wall and the Japanese men talked among themselves. I stood silently at attention. Almost before I
knew it, I had been dismissed and was on my way
back to Shed 8.

"Lilian," I said as I entered the room, "certainly
there are spies among us. What do you think?"

"Yes, there must be," she agreed. "These bamboo
walls seem to have ears."

From that time on, any serious talking was done
in the open spaces, not always easy because open
spaces were scarce at Kampili Camp.

Lilian and I tried to stay together as much as our

work would permit. A slight lady to begin with, Lilian was becoming noticeably thin and frail. Her weight, I would guess, was down to about 60 pounds. Lilian worked with the cooking crew. Her special job was making porridge for sick people. The doctor prescribed for her the privilege of licking out the drums after the porridge was served. That privilege provided her a little extra nourishment. Despite her physical frailty, Lilian's sweet and quiet spirit always shone through.

A special blessing came about this time. Outside, along the length of our shed, was a ditch into which we threw our waste water. Some seeds started to sprout there and three little plants began to grow. Soon, much to our surprise, we saw some small, knotty tomatoes about the size of walnuts. No prize winners, those 33 little tomatoes, but they were delicious to us at a time when we had very little to eat with our rice.

Two months after its first appearance, the black limousine entered the camp again. Everyone stood watching in hushed groups as Margaret, Philoma and Darlene stepped out.

They looked thin and haggard, pain and suffering etched into their emaciated faces. Darlene's hair had turned white. We welcomed the prisoners back, but there was no outward show of emotion as we didn't know how the Japanese would react. In our hearts, though, we were very thankful to see the women alive.

As Darlene came across the grounds from the commander's office, I went to meet her.

We walked arm-in-arm between the two sheds. I

had so many questions to ask, but I knew that it would not be wise.

Finally I said, "Are you all right, Darlene?"

She hesitated, then said, "I think things will be all right."

Her head was down. She did not look at me. I felt, rather than saw, the agony. (See *Evidence Not Seen* by Darlene Deibler Rose for a recounting of her experiences.)

Darlene continued to be withdrawn. Margaret and Philoma had both become mentally unbalanced. We learned that Margaret had been beaten many times. She was put in the hospital and given what special treatment was available. Everyday I went to feed her her meals. Almost as soon as she had eaten she would ask, "When are they going to give me something to eat?"

As the days passed, Margaret improved slowly. Lilian was her constant companion and guide.

Philoma had contracted a stubborn infection in an open wound on her buttocks. Soap and water were all we had to treat the wound. Her mental state did not improve. She was in very sad shape.

I began to realize that the horrible, terrifying experience that had precipitated these tragic results would have been mine, too, had I not traveled on a Canadian passport.

Another enemy attacked the camp: scavenger, rabies-infested dogs that frequently jumped the fences into the compound at sundown. The dogs prowled around looking for prey, especially when we had air raids night and day. The commander gave us special instructions on how to protect ourselves and permission to carry sticks to ward the dogs off. But sticks were scarce—they were all needed for firewood.

The first rabies catastrophe involved a six-year-old boy whose mother had befriended me when I was in the hospital. He was her only son. He had received only a slight scratch on the elbow, but that was enough for the deadly virus from the dog's saliva to enter his body.

With no medicine to work with, the doctors tried desperately to help the child by washing the wound with soap and water and then burning the flesh. All to no avail. The boy died a few weeks later, frothing at the mouth.

The boy's mother was the daughter of former Dutch missionaries in the Indies. She wanted nothing to do with Christianity and would not have a service of any kind for her child. He was simply buried with his tin cup. Two years earlier, her newborn infant had died when the Japanese invaded Malino.

Toos Hoogeveen was a beautiful young woman with a beautiful character to match. Her mother was the daughter of a former king of the island of Bali and her father was a Dutchman. One dark night when an air raid was in progress, Toos entered the trench shelter with others from her shed. When one of the rabid dogs approached the prisoners, they tried to fight it off with sticks. Toos bravely fought the dog, preventing it from entering the trench and holding it while another woman killed it with a knife. Her actions prevented many others in the trench from being hurt, but she herself was scratched and bitten.

Without proper treatment for rabies, Toos knew she was doomed. She asked to be isolated, knowing that a terrible death would come to her in anywhere from two to 12 weeks. Miss DeJong, a Salvation Army friend, cared for her until the end in a small house at the edge of the old camp. Long after her death, the people of the camp remembered Toos for her selfless courage.

Kampili Camp, in one way or another, continued to claim its victims.

10

Not Somehow, but Victorious

"Be still, and know that I am God:
I will be exalted among the heathen,
I will be exalted in the earth."
(Psalm 46:10)

Our nocturnal excursions to the trenches were becoming more frequent. One memorable night I will never forget for two reasons. The first was the length of the stay—we remained in the trenches until the early hours of the morning. All the while, we could hear the sounds of planes and in the distance, bombs falling. Finally all was quiet. It had been a tense six hours.

The second memory of that night is a precious one. As daybreak was approaching, off to the east of the camp, the sky lit up behind the line of trees and mountain ranges. We could not figure out what was causing the light. Were the villages burning from the bombing? Was it a forest fire? Who or what was causing this phenomenon?

The sky continued to brighten. Suddenly, as we

watched in wonder, a bright star—the morning star—appeared on top of the mountain. I thought of the Scripture about the morning stars singing together. I could almost see them in my mind's eye. I thought of Christ being described as the bright and morning star and remembered His promise to never leave us nor forsake us. God had not forgotten us. He knew where we were. He knew about each one of us.

One day, American planes came over dropping tin cans with a fuel tank attached. We thought it was a warning that they were planning to bomb the area. It had been rumored that the Japanese had been ordered to move everything that should not be bombed to within a radius of 20 miles of Makassar. Our camp was well within that radius. The rumors also reported that we would be held as hostages. It was hard to know what to believe. Some of it we didn't want to believe.

On July 17, 1945, the air raid siren sounded again. I was at my sewing machine working with the other women. We all jumped up and ran into the covered air raid shelter nearby. Low-flying planes rained silver incendiary bombs. One hit the end of our shelter and the bamboo support caught on fire. We all stampeded out the other end. Women and children were screaming and running helter-skelter. Most of them were heading toward the outer gate.

I started running, too, but I didn't know where to go. Fortunately, our shed was on the way to the front gate. I stopped at Shed 8, which miraculously was still standing, grabbed my emergency bag and

Bible off the foot of the bed and kept running.

I soon caught up with Mrs. Lie, a Chinese lady from Shed 8, who was struggling with her two small children. I swung one of them on my back and together we ran toward the gate.

The gate was open, so we kept running until we came to the edge of the jungle. I looked back toward Kampili and saw the Japanese lining the ditches, firing their machine guns at the American planes as the incendiary bombs fell all around. Fortunately, not all the bombs went off. Nevertheless, the camp was ablaze in no time.

Someone shouted, "There's a river in this direction," so we all headed off in that direction.

When the bombing and shooting stopped and the air raid was over, I found myself at the dry river bed with a few others, most of whom I did not know. The Japanese herded us back into the destroyed camp.

Not one of the 16 sheds nor any other bamboo buildings were left. The only structures remaining were the commander's headquarters, the cement base of the main kitchen and a few cement houses in the Ambon section. The camp had burned like a matchbox.

Soon, Japanese soldiers were pouring into the camp in great numbers to make sure we did not escape. They also brought several ambulances and seemed prepared to set up a Red Cross base. Five lives were lost and several were injured that day.

I later learned that Mrs. Jaffray had been in an open trench when the bombing took place. Margaret Jaffray had been in another one nearby. The lady next to Margaret was injured so badly that her leg had to amputated. Margaret, thankfully, escaped with only a grazed toe.

The first one of our group that I saw was Darlene. We walked back to the shed that had been our home for two years to see if there was anything left to salvage. We found nothing except some burned forks. Even the metal motto that I kept on top of my suitcase—"Not somehow, but victorious"—was gone. But the principle remained. We were not just to get through this horror somehow, but we were to emerge victorious. That we were determined to do.

Strangely enough, a papaya tree that had self-sown in the ditch beside our shed was still upright. We had been waiting for the fruit on it to ripen, but the burning building had cooked it. We ate it. How good it tasted! It provided us nourishment for another day.

11

Jungle Home

*"I had fainted, unless I had believed to see the
goodness of the LORD in the land of the living."
(Psalm 27:13)*

It was July 17, 1945. Shortly after we returned
to the burned-out camp, we were once again
ordered to "pigi," this time to a place about half
a mile away. We had heard that something was
being built in the jungle. Now we knew this place
was for us.

For this jungle journey, unlike our earlier one
from Benteng Tinggi, we didn't have much to
carry—it had all been destroyed. All I had left was
my emergency bag containing a dress, a housecoat,
two pillow slips, a piece of a towel, needle, thread
and scissors, an address book and my passport and
Bible.

With the allies closing in, the Japanese became
extremely angry and frustrated and began making
radical changes in the personnel of the camp.

Mrs. Joustra, the kind Dutch lady who had been
in charge of the camp under Commander Yamaji,
either asked to be relieved of her responsibilities or

was fired. She had served well and with much wisdom.

Mrs. Bartstra was then assigned the difficult job, but she lasted only a short time. For some reason, unknown to us and perhaps to her, she was ordered to go out and dig her own grave. We never knew the reason for this. After digging for a while, again for some unknown reason, she was ordered to stop.

Next, Darlene was ordered to be the leader. She tried to tell Yamaji that she wasn't capable or clever enough.

His reply was, "You don't have to be clever. Just do what I say." What a position for Darlene to be in, especially after her solitary confinement experience in Makassar.

Apparently Yamaji had confidence in Darlene, or was it as Lilian correctly observed that the move was political? If the rumor that the allies were near and we would be held hostages was true, it would have been a good move on the part of Yamaji to put an American in charge of the camp. But Darlene was later released from the job and Mrs. Bartstra was reinstated.

Our new jungle home was made up of many little bamboo and reed buildings less than half the size of those in Kampili Camp. But at least we had a roof over our heads, four walls and a slat floor to sleep on. The houses rested on poles about three feet up from the ground. This allowed plenty of damp air to come up from below. From above, the buildings were well sheltered by big trees and thick jungle growth.

When the time came to assign people to the

buildings, those of us from Shed 8 asked to stay together. We had been through both joys and sorrows together and we also loved our shed leader, Darlene. Mrs. Jaffray and Margaret continued to live back at Kampili Camp in the Ambon area in one of the cement houses that was unharmed during the air raid. All their belongings had survived the attack. Philoma Seely was also at the Ambon Camp. Physically she had improved, but mentally she remained critical.

The sleeping spaces in our new jungle home were measured out according to our number. With 100 of us that meant that we each had 17 inches of floor space. That really was quite ample, because by this time, most of us fit very well in 17 inches! I am five feet, four inches and I estimate that at that time I weighed about 80 pounds. Nevertheless, we felt like sardines packed in a can.

The close quarters did help to keep us warm, for we had no blankets or mosquito nets. When I say we had lost everything, that is exactly what happened—we had truly lost everything except what we had on our backs (and, of course, what I had in my emergency bag).

Somewhere, somehow, Darlene acquired a piece of blanket. (I later learned that Margaret Jaffray had divided her only blanket into three sections: one for Darlene and me, one for Lilian and Margaret and one for her mother and herself.) In the dark, Darlene offered to share it with me. Was I ever surprised the next morning when I saw the size of it! It was about four feet long by two-and-a-half feet wide!

"Darlene," I exclaimed, "I am so sorry! Is this all there is to it?" I had assumed that the blanket was bigger and had kept pulling on it trying to cover myself during the night.

Each day brought more difficult problems. An atmosphere of impending doom settled over the camp. What was ahead, we did not know, but it was sure to be worse than what we had already experienced. The question was—would we survive? Surely it would take a miracle!

Although my blue *Hymns of the Christian Life* was destroyed in the bombing, the messages of many of the songs often came to mind. One seemed particularly appropriate for the situation:

> In the hour of trial, Jesus plead for me,
> Lest by base denial I depart from Thee
> When Thou seest me waver, with a look recall;
> Nor for fear or favor, Suffer me to fall.

On July 19, 1945, two days after the first bombing and now in the new camp, the air raid siren screamed again. This time we laid face down on the ground and covered our heads with our hands. Heavy shrapnel bombs were being dropped on the old camp. Though we were half a mile away, we could feel the ground heave underneath us with every strike. Even from that distance we could see the big craters that were left in the ground.

Our daily chores included clearing the ground around the camp of layers of jungle leaves, dead branches, and all kinds of creatures—lizards, bugs, snakes, bats, rats and a wide assortment of mosquitos and other insects. In the process, a stick grazed my right leg above the ankle. The small wound developed into an ugly tropical ulcer. Many people already had such sores, but I had escaped up to this point.

A banyan tree with large, extensive roots grew not far from our hut. We often sat between its roots. We also took shelter there during air raids—until one day, when out of the corner of my eye, I saw something moving overhead. Curious, I stepped back to get a better look.

"Margaret! Lilian! Come out!" I shouted, trying not to frighten them unduly. A 10-foot-long snake was slithering across the vines and branches toward the trunk. The snake had obviously swallowed something, because it had a protrusion in its middle. There was no telling how many more snakes claimed this territory. We had to live and let live, hoping they would do the same.

Food and water were still being carried from the old camp. The kitchen had burned, but the drums that sat on the cement platform were still usable. There were no pigs left to tend. They had burned along with their sheds. The food supply was very sparse, barely subsistence level. In the morning we were served hot water or coffee. Then, in the afternoon, we had our meal for the day—a mixture of rice porridge, *sayur litchin* (the slippery vegetable), and pork—the remnants of Kampili Camp.

Each woman had to take her turn going back to the old camp to do various jobs so we would have food and water. A water brigade was formed that stretched between the well and the improvised kitchen. Where all the pails came from was a puzzle to me. Perhaps they were from the pig pens. We had used equally undesirable tin cans in the past.

After the water was drawn from the well with a pail and rope, it was dumped into another pail which the first lady carried about 30 feet to the second lady, and so on. It took about 20 women to reach the kitchen drums. The efficiency of the system was rather doubtful. So much water was spilled along the way that by the time a pail reached its destination, it was only half full.

All was calm one day as I finished my turn on the water gang. I had just started my lone walk back to the jungle camp when the alarm sounded. I was walking through a large, open, desert-like space, with no place to take shelter. I ran as fast as I could toward a fence with bushes behind it.

Just then the plane flew directly overhead. I tried to climb over the fence, but got caught in the barbed wire. Fortunately, no bombs dropped that day. I gratefully picked myself off the barbed wire and continued my walk back to the jungle.

In addition to the shortage of food, we had very little water and no soap. All the clothes we had were on our backs. It was very difficult to keep clean. However, with my emergency bag and Bible, grabbed before Shed 8 burned, I had more items than most of the women—a comb, a pair of pillow slips with tatting on the edge, a piece of Turkish towel and scissors which Darlene and I used to cut each other's hair.

One day, my young friend, Mien Van de Haarst,

asked if she could borrow my comb. No one in their family of five had a comb. They were trying to comb their long hair with burned forks. My first thought was to say no because she had lice. But the Lord prompted me to loan her the comb. I never got lice, nor did anyone else among the eight or 10 people who used that comb.

Rabid dogs continued to plague us. More people in our camp died from dog bites than were killed by bombs. Everyone had some sickness—dysentery, malaria, beri beri, tropical ulcers, skin diseases, hydrophobia or mental illness.

For a while, funerals were held every day. The graveyard was filling fast. Rev. Spreeuwenberg, the Dutch missionary who had served all this time in the women's camp as handyman and preacher, performed his job faithfully day after day. In my mind, I can still see him standing there in the pouring rain, trying to give a word of encouragement to the crowd of 50 to 100 gathered at the graveside.

The Japanese were becoming more and more unpredictable. First, they would do us a favor, then, without provocation, they would punish us for some imaginary shortcoming. It appeared that we would indeed be used as hostages.

12

Free at Last!

"Bless the LORD, O my soul: and all that is within me, bless his holy name."
(Psalm 103:1)

We had had no news from the outside world for four long years. And now, with threatening signs on the one hand and encouraging ones on the other, a thousand questions once again whirled around in our minds. Was the report true? Had the Japanese really surrendered? Were the Americans coming? Would freedom include us? Were our husbands still alive? What would happen next? Would this dreadful imprisonment soon be over?

Rumor was that the war was over. In fact the Japanese had announced it. Part of me dared to dream it might be so. Another part recoiled at the thought of possible unfulfilled hope.

On September 4, 1945, American planes flew over the camp dropping leaflets. The leaflets read: "Medicines and other articles will be dropped tomorrow to internees. Mark an area 150 by 50 meters in or near the camp, with a cross in the center. A small committee should be formed to distribute the supplies." Yamaji cooperated and carried out the instructions. He had had a conference with the Australians in Makassar, the Australians being the occupying forces in the area.

The very next day supplies were indeed dropped in big army bags. Some of them split open. The women and children went wild! Some chocolate rations dropped in the sand, but we ate them just the same. But, oh, my teeth! They ached from the sweetness. Our diet and lack of dental care for over five years had taken their toll.

The day the planes flew over (September 4th) dropping those leaflets, I had been sent by the Japanese with a group of 11 women (including a 10-year-old girl) to clean houses in Makassar, about 17 miles away. We made the trip standing in the back of a truck, wondering all the time what was in store for us. We were dropped off at a house on a street that was unfamiliar to me.

We parked in front of a nice stone structure. At the order to disembark and enter, we obeyed quickly and silently. We had had many lessons on how to "pigi."

The house had at one time been furnished nicely in traditional Dutch fashion. But evidently it had been occupied by Japanese officers and had been stripped of the furniture.

"Clean the house!" someone barked the order.

"Where are the cleaning utensils?" I asked as we followed one another through the house.

"There is nothing around here," Mrs. Snaith added, "no broom, no mop, nothing in the bathroom or kitchen."

I became suspicious. Could this just be a trick to deceive us? They had told us the war was over, but was it true?

We continued to investigate, looking behind doors and in corners. About the most exciting thing we found was a full length mirror on the bathroom door. What a shock!

"Ernie must never see me like this!" I exclaimed. My hair was plain and straggly and my face was all pimples. The Kampili green dress fit fairly well, but it sure could have been more becoming. The last touch was my bandaged right leg which still had the tropical ulcer.

A special treat was in store for us. Some Christians from the Gospel Tabernacle in another part of the city heard that we were there and brought a delicious Indonesian dinner all prepared and hot. How good it was to see them! How good the food tasted! We, of course, inquired about others and learned how gracious the Lord had been to them. The Christians did not stay long. Though arms were supposed to have been laid down, the populace was still nervous.

That evening, just before dark, a Japanese soldier surprised us at the door. He had come to summon us all to return to Kampili Camp. We hadn't done any cleaning, but we had had a fine dinner and a great outing in Makassar. This time we all piled into a car with the soldier driving.

Before we reached the camp, the car broke down. In the penetrating darkness all around us, the driver got out of the car and lit a match. We wondered what kind of trouble we were in! Fortunately, with some tinkering under the hood, the driver got the car running before too long and we were on our way again.

With a sense of relief, we reached Kampili with its reassurance of a protected area. The Japanese chauffeur took us to a cement building in the Ambon section and we spent the rest of the night sleeping on the tile floor.

In these momentous days of transition between the Japanese and the Australians, Darlene and I did not see much of each other. She was spending a lot of time with Yamaji and other authorities at the camp headquarters helping to interpret for visitors who came to the camp.

On September 8th, I was appointed, along with several other women, to return to Makassar. We were assigned to a small duplex at 62 Bessieweg. We entered the house cautiously, looked around and each one chose a bedroom.

The rooms were bare, but at least it was a house with more protection than our jungle dwelling had afforded. The room I chose had a single mattress on the floor and one pillow. No mosquito nets. We were not there to clean—we were there to greet our husbands when they returned from Pare Pare!

September 9th. A truck came to the house three times to distribute food and to give each one of us a soup spoon, a cup and a dish.

September 10th. The day was spent in prayer and praise and waiting. Waiting.

September 11th. Being sequestered in close quarters in this one residential area, we all heard the rumor—this was the day!

It wasn't long until Ernie was standing at the door. He looked taller than ever because he had lost so much weight. But he looked terrific to me! It had been three and a half years since we had seen each other.

He was dressed in internment clothes—a pair of shorts, no shirt and wooden *klombs*. I, too, was dressed in my Kampili outfit—a khaki skirt I had made in the sewing room and a blouse I made from two dish towels.

We stared at each other momentarily as he stood silhouetted in the doorway. A thought raced through my mind, *Oh my, doesn't he approve of me? Can't he accept me the way I am now?*

But the questions were fleeting. He wrapped his long arms around me and lifted me off my feet like he had always done.

"Thank the Lord we are together again!" he whispered gently.

"Yes, Lord. Thank You!" I nodded.

Hilarious days followed. Even the smallest things made us laugh. We were like two newlyweds on our honeymoon. Each morning, and at other times throughout the first few days, I found gifts on my pillow that Ernie had made out of water buffalo horns or wood. One day it was a table mat made out of wired together domino pieces which formed a diamond.

As far as Ernie was concerned, he was determined to make up for lost time. He made appointments with the Dutch and Australian officials including the Australian Red Cross. He wanted desperately to get to the Mission property and the homes of the Christians that were still in forbidden territory.

Mr. Snaith and Mr. Woodward had not yet arrived from Pare Pare. Their wives were getting anxious.

September 13th. Before we had finished our breakfast, Brigadier Woodward and Major Snaith arrived at the house. Another happy reunion! What joy filled our house during those days! We were also enjoying three good meals a day.

Ernie went out for a couple hours in the morning and returned at noon.

"I have some news for you, Ruth," he said. "We are moving across the street to 9 Bessieweg. It's a large house and will accommodate all the ladies as they come from Kampili. Are you ready?"

"Of course, I'm ready," I responded. There wasn't much to get ready—only my emergency bag. The only increase in my worldly goods was the gifts Ernie had given me, which included this morning's gift of about 20 drops of cologne—the last of Dr. Jaffray's many bottles.

We said goodbye to our friends and walked across the street, which was lined on one side with small houses and on the other with much larger ones.

As we entered 9 Bessieweg, I exclaimed, "Oh, this is like a palace compared to what we have lived in during the last few years!" A few shutters were broken, but otherwise the house was in good condition. It had a large living room, a dining area with a table and four chairs and three large bedrooms, all with beds.

The day was filled with one surprise after another. Gifts poured in from the Red Cross— mosquito nets, blankets, sheets, pillow cases. Food came daily. Each one of us received a box with a change of clothing and toiletries. Our Christian friends from the tabernacle and Bible school also stopped by. In addition to more food, they also brought our own clothes and other articles that they had been able to salvage for us.

Today's gift from Ernie was a pair of miniature *klombs* one-and-a-half inches long—a replica of the ones he had sent me in Kampili. The days were filled with spontaneous thanks to the Lord for His mercy and goodness to us. It was great to be alive—and together!

September 15th. Darlene, Lilian, Margaret, Philoma and Margaret Jaffray all arrived from Kampili. Mrs. Jaffray went to stay with some Chinese friends they had known from the Chinese church in Makassar. Also on this day the Union Jack was hoisted for the first time in more than a century over the Australian headquarters in Makassar.

September 16th—Sunday. We had English services in our living room.

September 19th. Margaret Kemp and Darlene left on a plane for America. It was a sad but joyous moment. We had shared these war years and so many difficult experiences. Our hearts were full of thankfulness to the Lord for His faithfulness to each one of us. Philoma remained in Makassar.

I found it especially difficult to say goodbye to

Darlene. To think that she had to return home without Russell was very sad. I almost felt guilty. Here I was, so happy here with Ernie and so grateful for the way things turned out for me. It was hard.

Ernie had lost one of the best friends he ever had when Russell died. Russell was friendly, kind, congenial and as our Dutch friend put it, "a diplomat." Ernie and Russell's friendship dated back to their days at the Missionary Training Institute in Nyack, New York. They had both applied for missionary service and were sent out together in 1930.

After Russell's marriage to Darlene and their return to the field, they had served among the stoneage tribes of the Wissel Lakes of Dutch New Guinea (now called Irian Jaya).

When Russell was appointed as assistant chairman of the field, he and Ernie were once again working side by side as Ernie was the head of the Bible school in Makassar at our headquarters. You have already read the story of how they were interned together in Pare Pare.

Ernie said that during the 17 months Russell lived in the camp, he endeared himself to all classes of men. When on August 19, 1943, he suddenly passed away, the feeling of loss was widespread. He was only 38 years old when God called him home.

September 22nd. We said goodbye to Lilian Marsh, Dr. Jaffray's secretary and faithful friend to his family, and to Mrs. Jaffray and Margaret. Once more, it was sad that Dr. Jaffray could not experience the joy of going home. His death had been so recent—only 17 days before the war ended. He had already gone "home."

Dr. Jaffray had been treated well and respected at Pare Pare. He was given a place where he could continue his exposition of the scriptures undisturbed. The first part of the internment had proven bearable and even when dysentery had taken down two-thirds of the occupants, Dr. Jaffray had remained well.

But after the bombing, the internees were forced to live outside in an area originally constructed for pigs. Dr. Jaffray became lethargic on only one-half pound of rice per day. He began to lose strength rapidly and on July 29th walked through the valley to his reward. (See "Appendix I" for details on the last days of Dr. Robert Jaffray.)

We could have gone home with Lilian and the others, but we chose to stay. Ernie, the only man out of our original missionary group, felt that he could not leave until new missionaries were sent to fill up the ranks. Blessed with good food and joyful hearts, we were gaining strength every day and looking forward to building on the foundation that had been so faithfully laid before the war.

Late in the afternoon on September 22nd, Walter and Viola Post arrived from New Guinea and moved in with us at 9 Bessieweg. The Posts had evacuated to Australia during the war. They brought a radio with them and it was then that we heard the news of the deaths of our Borneo missionaries—Rev. John Willfinger, Rev. and Mrs. Sande and Rev. Fred Jackson. They had all been killed by the Japanese during the first year of the war.

The Australians came to pick us up in Army trucks equipped with wicker chairs for us to sit on and transported us to a ship where they entertained us royally. It was difficult to believe that we were actually sitting in a dining room and eating a delicious Australian-American meal complete with fresh baked bread and ice cream. All those good things showered upon us had come so suddenly. Truly the Lord had prepared a bountiful table before us in the presence of our enemies.

As soon as the ban on the Mission area of town was lifted, Ernie lost no time in contacting students and workers from the Bible school and church. We held English church services in our home. Many Australians joined us. Once again we were aware of the bond that exists among believers in Christ. We were also able to retrieve many items that belonged to various missionaries and to the Mission—3,000 books, bookcases, safes and letter files. We were thankful, too, that our typewriter and sewing machine were returned. They were put to good use right away.

By October we were receiving regular Army rations of dried potatoes, cabbage, carrots, beets, meat and eggs. Bread was delivered daily.

We had received no letters from home in the two months that we had been free. The suspense increased by the day. What had happened to our families during all those years of crisis? It would be another two months—January of 1946—before we heard that our families were all fine.

Although free, we were unfortunately still marked people. Thieves lurked everywhere. One morning,

very early, we were stunned to discover the Posts'
radio was missing. We had heard no sounds of
prowlers in the night, but then, bare feet make very
little noise.

Thievery became almost a nightly occurrence. It
was impossible to lock up the house securely because it had many windows with open shutters.
We had no lights and tropical nights are inky black.

One night Ernie woke up suddenly to find a man
standing beside our bed. He let out a blood-curdling yell and the man ran for the front door, but
not before he grabbed a scarf off my bedside stand
and a couple of small rugs that the Christians had
returned to us. After that episode, Ernie went to
bed armed with a hammer!

A couple of nights later, a thief showed up again.
This time he tried entering through the window in
the Posts' room. First a hand appeared, then an
arm over the top window. Fortunately, he never got
in the house, probably having heard stirring inside.
Such was the aftermath of war!

In the midst of all this, I contracted a severe
case of dengue fever. Dengue fever is sometimes
called "breakbone fever," an accurate description
of the pain it causes. For five days I suffered. An
Australian doctor came to visit me and gave me
liquid aspirin. He said he had never seen such a
severe case.

I had a hemorrhagic rash from my neck down to
my feet. What a sight I was, especially when the
rash began to leave. I was black, blue and yellow all
over.

During those days Ernie often read to me, trying

to help me endure the physical pain and mental strain. I asked him to read the verses I had underlined in my Bible during my internment days, especially those in the book of Psalms. I had learned that the promises of God's Word could sustain me through the most difficult places. Once again, free but with this painful disease, His Word brought comfort and release to my heart.

13

The Journey

*"But they that wait upon the LORD shall renew
their strength; they shall mount up with wings
as eagles; they shall run, and not be weary;
and they shall walk, and not faint."*
(Isaiah 40:31)

Ernie felt that the time had come to make
every effort to find out what had happened
to the workers and the work that he had
pioneered in East Borneo and served for so many
years.

Certain things we already knew—Fred Jackson,
the Sandes and John Willfinger were gone.

Rev. Fred Jackson had arrived in Netherlands
East Indies in 1941 and became the pilot of the
Mission plane. With the onslaught of the war in the
Pacific, the Dutch government asked permission to
use the plane. The Mission left the choice up to
Fred. He chose to serve by conveying the sick and
wounded out of the jungle and carrying mail and
other messages. It was a hazardous undertaking because the hydroplane was slow and unarmed.

In January of 1942, Jackson and the Sandes were

evacuated to the interior of Borneo along with 120 Dutch and British refugees. They lived in a house near a Dyak Christian village across the river from the government post. All was well until August 20, 1942, when the Japanese suddenly appeared and quickly overpowered the garrison.

A few days later, approximately 40 men, including Fred Jackson and Andrew Sande, were killed. About one month later, Mrs. Sande, baby David and all white women were also killed.

Rev. John Willfinger had been in his fourth year as a missionary in the interior of Borneo at Long Berang (where Ernie had pioneered) when the Japanese took over. The Dyak Christians wanted to hide John and keep him safe from the invaders, but he chose to give himself up rather than cause them to lie and put the Dyaks' lives in jeopardy. The Japanese had already threatened death to any native who would hide a white man.

John sent the following letter (printed here in part) to The Honorable Mr. Singal, at Long Berang:

If I hide, naturally the saints will be forced to lie and to disobey orders if they hide me. In short, I would be forced to drag them into sin, whereas my intention upon leaving my country and my family was only to make mankind righteous and not to bring them into sin, even though I pay for it with my life.

In short, sir, because of Jesus Christ and His sheep, before I will do anything whatsoever that is not right, I surely will surrender myself. May my Saviour be with me as He promised in Mat-

*thew 28:19–20. Until now He has been with me
and I know that He will be with me until the
end. Therefore this is my decision.*

On Christmas Eve, 1942, John was killed with a
bayonet, beheaded and buried in a shallow grave.
He was 32 years old.

Miss Grace Dittmar had escaped from her station in Sumatra to Java. She managed to catch one
of the last ships to the United States. The vessel
was crowded and the accommodations were poor.
As a result of exposure and sickness, Grace went to
be with the Lord about two months after she arrived in America.

Ernie's real burden was to get back to Long
Berang where he had begun his ministry 13 years
before. We had already heard about Americans
being helped by the Christian Dyaks in the Long
Berang area before we left Makassar.

A sailor named Jim and some other Americans,
we were told, were flying over Borneo in the early
years of the war. Their plane was shot down by the
enemy. After they crashed, the Nipponese pilots
strafed them, killing five of the men. Only four
boys were left. They ended up in Long Berang
where "Bill" Presswood had lived.

They told how that except for the kindness of the
Christian natives they would all have died. They
had also received a strong witness through the
nightly meetings. (After this group returned to
America, they sent bolts of material to be dis-
tributed to the Dyaks. One Dyak, in appreciation,
sent a vase to a Lt. Philip Cory in California.)

Ernie wanted to see for himself. We headed toward Long Berang. Ernie's account of our trip is as follows:

For some time we had been feeling that a start should be made in contacting the workers and work in the various districts where the Alliance carried on missionary work before the war. With a prayer in our hearts for guidance, we wended our way on the morning of November 20 to the Australian headquarters with the purpose of inquiring about the possibility of visiting some of our east Borneo mission fields.

Shortly after arriving, we began making inquiries about Rev. John Willfinger, who had been reported killed there by the Japanese. After some preliminary inquiries, we came in contact with Private Loupatty who had been with a party of interned soldiers working on the roads with a Japanese guard. They had found a piece of pyjama and were told by the guard that it was from an American missionary who had been killed there. Having learned the exact spot, I took a Dutch official and a doctor with a gang of workmen. After some fruitless search, we finally found a human skeleton. That these were the mortal remains of our dear Brother Willfinger, there can be no doubt whatever. His fountain pen with his name on it, along with other personal articles, gave us positive proof.

After the remains had been carefully examined to ascertain the cause of death, a funeral service was held. Two Australian chaplains took part

*and the writer spoke about the life and work of
our departed brother. Interment was made in the
European cemetery at Tarakan.*

November 20, 1945, turned out to be an eventful
day for me. Almost before I knew what was happening, we were flying in a Catalina to Borneo. We
landed at Balikpapan, a city on the east coast of
Borneo and spent the night in an Australian
military installation. Ernie bunked with the men
and I was assigned to the nurses' quarters—a tent
on a wooden platform.

Being all alone, I was terribly frightened, feeling
that something or someone was around me that
was not supposed to be. I crawled into bed with my
clothes on, pulled the covers over my head and
prayed, "Dear Lord, cover me with the protecting
blood of Jesus and keep me safe under Your wing."

In the morning, I said to one of the nurses, "A big
black dog came in my tent last night."

With a surprised look, she responded, "We don't
have any dogs around here." I have no idea to this
very day who or what was the owner of those
strange blue eyes! Whatever the circumstance, it
was not of God, but was from Satan—a display of
the powers of evil that pervaded that land.

The next day we were on the Catalina again,
flying to Tarakan. From the time we landed in
Tarakan, a small island off the coast of Borneo and
a gateway to East Borneo, I was both excited and
frightened. Ernie was familiar with the land and the
people, his first impressions having been formed
many years earlier. But with the dawning of each

new day and the setting of the sun, I was forming mine.

Tarakan itself had been destroyed during the war. The extent of the destruction was staggering. Huge oil storage drums stood twisted and distorted. Temporary bamboo buildings and quonset huts dotted the terrain.

We stayed in the government house that had a cement floor, leaf walls and a tin roof that magnified the sound of the rain drops pelting down.

We became acquainted with the Australian officials and chaplains (padres). They provided us with food, first aid supplies and bedding, including the ubiquitous mosquito net.

Ernie had several opportunities to speak to gatherings. At one particular meeting on the beach, the presence of the Lord was manifested. That night three men raised their hands to accept the Lord Jesus Christ as their personal Savior and promised to serve Him. One was Des Trindall.

Two years and eight months later, a letter arrived from Des Trindall in Sydney, Australia. He wrote, "For the first time, as far as I can remember, I heard the simple message of salvation along the little beach of Tarakan and I was awakened to my need of Christ."

Des Trindall returned home to prepare for missionary service. Other letters later arrived from his post in New Guinea. How good to know that there was fruit that remained from our witness!

It was reported that Japanese were still hiding in the jungles around Borneo. In addition, there was still not enough food and water. Ernie and I had lived dangerously for so long that it seemed to be our life style! We once again placed our trust in the living God to direct and keep us.

There was considerable delay in receiving permission, but after about two weeks we were permitted to go to the Bulongan district. We contacted four of our national workers and arranged to revisit the area when the pastors had had time to assemble.

Most boats and travel vehicles used after the war had been salvaged from the bottom of the sea. Even if you could get permission to travel, it was very hard to find transportation. Finally, permission came for us to travel to Tanjungselor, a village across the bay from Tarakan.

We arrived at the Tarakan wharf expecting to depart as scheduled. After we had waited several hours, however, the boatman decided not to go that day after all. No explanation was offered, but given the superstitions of that area, it was probably because the birds were not flying in the right direction, a bad omen for undertaking such a trip.

"Perhaps we are not supposed to go on this trip," I said wearily as we tried to plan what to do next.

Ernie's comment was, "Oh yes, this is Satan's tactic."

We finally arrived in Tanjungselor. Ernie had been right—the delay was Satan's tactic—for immediately we felt the powers of darkness pressing upon us. We had permission to stay in the government house, but the keeper didn't seem to want us there. He even shot off a gun—whether for our benefit or someone else's we didn't know. That night we took turns reading the Scriptures aloud and praying. A battle was raging in the heavenlies and we knew it. Only God could help us.

At daybreak, we were awakened by men pounding on the doors and shouting. If Ernie knew what they were saying, he didn't tell me. I knew only that he was troubled. Perhaps it was because we were white. Perhaps it was the reaction of religious fanatics of the area to what we stood for. I never did find out.

While in Tanjungselor, we had an opportunity to pay a visit to the Sultan, who had been reinstated after being a common farmer for the period of the Japanese occupation. Fortunately for us, the NICA gave us rations to take with us to Bulongan, for prices of goods ranged up to 20 times pre-war prices.

After Ernie had made arrangements for a conference with the national teachers to be held the last week of January, we went back to Tarakan. By this time, some of the Dutch were returning to their posts. Even some women had returned. The Australians were preparing to return home. It was time for the Dutch to once again take over the authority of the land.

Malinau village stretched along the Sesayap River for about one mile. The Dutch government had an outpost there.

During the waiting days in Malinau, Ernie often referred to his pocket notebook which he carried at all times trying to obtain information about people he knew. Sesayap was where Ernie had made his first headquarters in 1932. He and Walter Post had made long and rigorous trips up the river's tributaries, searching out dozens of hidden villages in the mountainous jungle.

The Dyaks, although known as the wildest of the wild and restrained from headhunting only by government intervention, responded spontaneously and in great numbers to the gospel. Thousands had come to know Christ as their Savior. But at what a price!

One day I asked Ernie why he was always in such a hurry and encouraged him to relax a bit more.

His response was, "I guess I've heard too many messages on redeeming the time. I don't want to waste time."

We celebrated Christmas in Malinau, but there wasn't much to remind us of Christmas—no beautiful carols, no gifts, no cards or letters. In fact, we still had not heard any word from friends and family in America. Four long years of silence.

We ate our chicken and rice dinner outdoors on a crude wooden table. The only bright spot was three gorgeous red hibiscus that I picked from a nearby bush.

The day finally came when, seated in the center of a long Dyak dugout canoe, we were bound for Long Berang. It was a scorching day. This part of Borneo is very near the equator. I was thankful for the big straw hat I had purchased.

All our baggage was packed securely in the dugout canoe, the famous vehicle of Borneo rivers. The boat was 40 feet long, with boards secured dovetail fashion by rattan. The widest part of the boat in the center was three-and-one-half feet across and tapered at each end to travel swiftly through narrow passageways or rocks and rapids. Such a boat held about 1,600 pounds.

One hour into this canoe trip, I had had enough! And a whole day of travel was still before us!

We swayed from side to side, trying to keep the canoe in balance as the natives paddled. In deep water, six or eight men maneuvered the canoe by standing on the top edges and paddling. When the water was only three or four feet deep, the men poled with long bamboo poles. When the current was very strong, rattan ropes were tied to the front and back of the boat. Two Dyaks jumped out, swam to the river bank, ropes in tow, and walked along the precarious shoreline holding tightly to the ropes to prevent the boat from being lost to the strong current.

Our first day's journey finally came to an end.

I said, "Oh, this is great to finally get out of the boat!" A couple of minutes later, however, I wasn't so sure—I was land sick after all the swaying. I walked up the river bank to the Dyak long house, all the time praying for strength and balance.

My next challenge was to climb a notched pole up into the long house I had heard so much about. Dyak long houses are built on stilts 10 feet above the ground. Boats and other things are stored underneath. The notched pole measured about 15 feet long and seven inches wide, with notches chipped out for toe holds. The pole leaned against the house at the doorway and was usually pulled in for the night. Still swaying from the day in the dugout, I miraculously made it up the pole.

With one quick glance I sized up our resting

place for the night. At one end was a crude fireplace. Cooking pots and articles of cloth and leather hung from the roof on rattan cords, well out of reach of the many dogs the Dyaks kept.

In the opposite corner from the fireplace sat a large rice liquor jar with a long bamboo stem.

For everything we did, we had an audience. While we prepared for the night, the Dyaks chattered back and forth, amazed that "the men do all the work." Of course, in their culture, the women do all the work.

About 25 men, women and children slept on the floor on mats. About the same number of dogs roamed around the room. Now and then someone shouted at or kicked a dog. The dog would yelp, but never seemed to learn from the intended discipline.

A wood fire burned in the fireplace most of the night, casting an eerie shadow over the long house walls. From time to time people would get up and drink from the liquor jar.

The only spot for our two camp cots was near the doorway. That arrangement suited us fine. Our clothes, shoes, sneakers— anything loose—we slept on to keep them away from the dogs.

I collapsed wearily onto my cot, but all night I clung to the edges, for it felt like it was swaying back and forth as the canoe had done all day. At my head, two chickens roosted comfortably.

The next morning, I awoke feeling unusually well. I was very thankful, for another day's journey lay before us.

Once again, we settled into the dugout. The

Ruth Brooks, 1933.

Dr. Robert A. Jaffray.

Ernest Presswood, about 1930.

Ernest and Ruth Presswood before they left for Borneo, 1941.

Dyaks with Guru Tondak.

Easter crowd at Long Berang.

House that Ernie built at Long Berang.

The Presswoods' first home in Makassar.

Ernie baptizing a believer in the Sesayap River.

A Dyak longhouse.

John Willfinger (left) and
Russell Deibler, 1938.

Rining (left) and Dawat. It
was Dawat whom the
Presswoods met coming
down the river from
Long Berang.

Shooting the rapids.

A memorial service for John Willfinger, December 1945. Just over a month later, Ernie was buried beside him.

September 1945, dressed in internment camp clothes. From left to right: Lilian Marsh, Margaret Jaffray, Ernie Presswood, Ruth Presswood, Philoma Seeley. Darlene Deibler and Margaret Kemp had already been repatriated.

Ruth and Ernie at No. 9 Bessieweg.

Margaret Kemp and Lilian Marsh after the war.

Ready to head upriver to Long Berang, 1945. The woman wearing the white hat in the last canoe is Ruth.

The house where
Ernie died.

The last picture of Ernie
and Ruth together.

Ruth with the group of Dyak students placed in her care after Ernie's death.

Darlene Deibler and Ruth,
taken after World War II.

Ruth's sewing class at the Makassar Bible School, taken after Ruth returned from Borneo alone, 1946.

Dyaks made the trip interesting with their whooping and yelling. The biggest commotion arose when a wild pig or some other animal came into view on the riverbank. They would make a beeline for it as we hung on for dear life. Their goal was to spear the animal or kill it with a blow gun.

The Sesayap River was infested with crocodiles. I was told that they stayed in the calm waters below the rapids. It was amazing how stealthily the crocodiles glided in the deep water.

After three days of traveling in calm water and staying in exotic places at night, we arrived at the first big rapid. The roar of the water from a distance reminded me of the sound of Niagara Falls. The boulders and waves that formed the rapids were enormous. For some, we stayed in the canoe. For others, we climbed out and crawled along the variegated rock wall covered with jungle vines. Meanwhile, the Dyaks unloaded the canoe and portaged it and the baggage around the rapid. Portaging was a time-consuming necessity.

The Dyaks were very skilled in navigating the rapids. The headman stayed at the back of the canoe and steered with an oar. The other men poled in and out of the water, cooperating with one another as they followed the headman's commands. The orders from the headman were given with great authority and in a loud voice so that he could be heard above the roar of the water. The men holding and pulling the rattan ropes had to be especially nimble, jumping over logs and maneuvering around large, slippery boulders.

Sometimes, rattan ropes in hand, the Dyaks had

to swim a distance until they could find a place to stand in order to pull on the canoe. The risks were high—there were snakes in the grass, the rattan ropes might break, the canoe could get stuck on a rock, or the men might fall and injure themselves.

It was usually a four-day trip through the rapids. Our stop at Semamu, up a side tributary, gave me a welcome break from the canoe. The Chinese merchant there opened up a crude "home" (actually a kind of lean-to added on to their storage area). At least we had boards to place our cots on.

Sandwiched between sacks of rice and other strange items, we had a good night's sleep. This was much better than sleeping along the river bank with the rising water flowing underneath us during the night!

Ernie tried on several occasions to witness to these people, but he was interrupted every time. The last evening in Semamu, Ernie tried again. Just then, a man from the upper part of the Island of Celebes walked in. He had been a Dutch government representative in this area before the war. Now, he had orders to report to the Dutch headquarters in Tarakan. The man seemed friendly enough, but Ernie was concerned.

"I don't trust this man," he told me. "I heard it was he who ordered John Willfinger to report to the Japanese." We were informed later that the Dutch had indeed imprisoned the man in Tarakan.

We left Semamu after a few bargaining procedures and the usual delays. The first night we camped in a very crude place at the edge of the jungle. Two of the Dyaks stayed with us and the others slept down on the pebbles at the river bank. They played their bamboo flutes far into the night to keep the evil spirits away.

Certainly the evil spirits needed to be kept away, but only the power and presence of Christ could do that.

14

"Home" at Long Berang

"Go ye therefore, and teach all nations,
baptizing them in the name of the Father,
and of the Son, and of the Holy Ghost."
(Matthew 28:19)

The last day's trip was very special as we neared Long Berang. Every so often the Dyak men gave their native call. Within a few minutes, a Dyak long house appeared in the distance and its occupants answered the call. Then the headman of our canoe would call, "Come! Come! Come see! Come meet our old teacher, the missionary!"

News spread quickly from one long house to another. By the time we reached the next long house, the occupants had strolled down to the river's edge. (Stroll is the correct word—nobody hurries in the jungles of Borneo!). We shook hands with each one, exchanging the usual greetings. This procedure continued at frequent intervals along the river until we reached Long Berang. Ernie was not sure how many people we would find still living in Long Berang. Many, they said, had built houses downstream.

Finally, after seven long days in the canoe, we arrived at the path that led from the river to the village of Long Berang. It was New Year's Day, 1946. I climbed cautiously out of the canoe and crawled along fallen trees to the shore. I felt a little dizzy and wondered why they couldn't have had a bigger log there. As it was, my foot slipped and I got one of my sneakers wet.

Many people were at the edge of the river to meet us. We shook hands with each one. Greetings out of the way, we headed down the path with the dugout crew following single file close behind with the baggage.

The path was well beaten but narrow. There were no such things as roads in these parts—the river was the road. The thought crossed my mind that this village was the wildest place I had ever seen. Ernie felt right at home, but I felt very strange with everybody staring at me.

We headed toward a cluster of buildings and reported to the head man. Beside us were little stores made of bamboo. There the Chinese traded, using rice as currency.

Dirt, flies and filth were everywhere. Fierce looking men dressed only in loin cloths and parangs (long knives). Women with long black hair in topless skirts. Naked children with runny noses.

I knew, however, that in spite of all my eyes were seeing and my mind was finding difficult to accept, that these were souls for whom Christ died. Already thousands of them had come to faith in the Lord Jesus Christ and their lives had been changed.

As we walked through the village, past the church building, a couple of Chinese stores and other assorted dwellings, it was obvious that we were in the heart of the wilds of Borneo.

The thought flashed through my mind, *If it's like this now, what was it like 13 years ago when Ernie first brought the gospel to these Dyaks?* I dared not dwell on the sacrifices that had already been made here in Long Berang and throughout all of Borneo to bring the good news to these people. Instead, I concentrated on the harvest of souls that had believed and were new creations in Christ Jesus.

We continued walking until we reached the other side of the village, where we were confronted by high stairs which took us up to the swinging bridge that spanned the second of the three rivers that met at Long Berang. This river flowed around the side and front of the Mission house.

The house had been hewn out of the jungle, built by Chinese carpenters who had proven difficult to hire and keep on the job. Ernie was a good carpenter, so he had supervised the work. People from America had sent some supplies, but for the most part, the job had been done the hard way—hewing lumber from the trees of the forest, waiting and more waiting for supplies from faraway places, daily problems with reluctant and recalcitrant workers.

Much love and patience and persistence had gone into this house. Now it was in shambles. We walked around the house and looked in every room, so obviously abused, and listened to the stories of what had taken place within its walls in the intervening years.

"Now we know why so many have moved away from Long Berang and built smaller long houses downstream," Ernie commented.

The Japanese had made the house their home and had waged guerilla war using it as a base. They had stored tons of rice there. Three Japanese men had been killed there. Old blood still stained the walls.

Ernie tried to obtain information about the work, the workers and the national Christians. Not understanding the Dyak language, I just observed and continued to learn what I could.

Something exciting seemed to be happening most of the time. As each of these "happenings" developed, we certainly knew it, for the Dyaks would whoop, yell and carry on in a frenzy. Soon, I did what everyone else did—I headed in the direction of the noise to see what was causing the commotion!

One day, several Dyaks came running heading up the river with their blow guns, knives and spears. Soon a large deer appeared in mid-stream. I looked at just the wrong time—as a spear pierced the animal's heart. They dragged the deer down into the water to bleed. This catch meant a feast for the people.

The Dyaks cooked their rice in an iron kettle and roasted their meat over an open fire. Fruits and vegetables were eaten raw. Banana leaves served as dishes—no dishwashing needed. And, of course, at every meal, we were well aware that fingers were made before forks.

The religion of the Dyaks was animistic. It ruled
their lives with fear and superstition and great
bondage. They had so many superstitions to follow.
If the birds flew in a certain way, they were not
supposed to plant, harvest, travel, bury the dead,
etc. They tied rattan knots in trees to hold the evil
spirits. In one place, they worshipped a big
crocodile made out of mud; in another, a big tree.
They tried to appease anything that gave them
trouble or that they did not understand. Even when
the Dyaks became Christians, the burden of their
customs weighed them down.

Women in Borneo had a difficult life. They took
care of the family, carried wood and water, cooked,
planted and harvested the rice fields. That, Ernie
explained, was why there were so few women and
children around in the village during the day. They
were in the fields.

Men had the "executive" jobs. They fished,
hunted, sold rice and traveled up and down the
rivers. They hunted and ate almost any kind of
animal, including snakes, birds, bats and insects.
Bats were considered a delicacy. But, oh, the horrible smell of them cooking!

At one village the Dyaks killed a python that had
swallowed a pig. That night, the people had both
snake and pig to eat—a double entree! The Dyaks
did not eat eggs. They would exclaim, "Wah! Look
how many chickens that would be!"

Dyak clothes, though few, were quite distinctive.
The men wore loin cloths or shorts and carried a
long knife at their side. The women and girls wore
a Malay sarong, wrapped around under their arms,

or a black apron-style skirt with or without a top. A little color was added to their wardrobe when servicemen parachuted into their area during the war. The women used the parachute material to make pretty yellow blouses.

The church services amazed me. They were performed Dyak fashion, but always with order. During prayer time, everyone prayed out loud, some louder than others. Then, suddenly, they all stopped. Had someone given a signal to stop? I couldn't tell. Most of the congregation were men. Their chatter and actions intrigued me.

One afternoon, I met with a group of Dyak women on the side porch of the house. A couple of the women spoke Malay, so a little communication was possible. Ernie had warned me, "Ruth, if they like you, don't be surprised if they put their hands on you. It's just their way of being friendly."

Sure enough, they touched me around my shoulders and neck, saying, "Boleh, boleh (May I? May I?)." I was glad I had been forewarned. Later, one of the women commented to Ernie, "Your wife is beautiful. She is small like we are."

My daily bath took place in the river. Usually a Dyak girl accompanied me. Like her, I washed myself under the sarong. Afterwards, we washed our clothes. I didn't linger in the river, for the water was ice cold. Also, there were many little fish five to six inches long that came to greet me. The greeting wasn't so bad, but when they started nipping me all over, I thought they had overdone their welcome.

Our day's activities started at sunrise and virtually stopped at sunset because our improvised lamps and flashlight gave very little light. A certain insect made a shrill noise on one note about 6 p.m. every evening. It became our signal for ending the day's work.

Night fell like a mammoth curtain around us. Being so close to the equator, there was no twilight—just light and within a few minutes, darkness.

Darkness! That's what Borneo was all about. Darkness—darkness of every kind.

15

Light in a Dark Place

"Therefore if any man be in Christ, he is a new
creature: old things are passed away;
behold, all things are become new."
(2 Corinthians 5:17)

One morning, as I was looking out the window, I saw Dyaks with their bamboo flutes gathering in a group in front of the house. Ernie called, "Ruth, come outside! The Dyak Christians want to welcome you!"

I realized a thrill similar to what John Willfinger must have experienced in 1939 when he first heard the music of the Dyaks. The bamboo flutes were graduated in size. The larger the flute, the lower the note. The narrower the flute, the higher the note. Although the bamboo band started off with a familiar hymn, I was soon reminded of the song called "The Lost Chord." Truly, this was a Borneo version of "The Lost Chord."

The conference began. As the reports were given, the problems mounted. There were many discouragements. Some workers had fallen into sin. But many had stood true, including Aris Doemat, one of the first five men to be ordained under the Alliance. He had remained the faithful leader in the area through the war years.

One matter of serious dispute was a heathen worship place—a large, bamboo altar to the evil spirits—that had been erected on the lawn of the Mission house. An animal had been sacrificed there and passed around to be eaten.

"The heathen altar to the evil spirits must come down!" Ernie declared. Some Christians were fearful, but with faith and courage in the Name of the Lord Jesus Christ, Ernie led those who were willing to destroy the structure.

One day a messenger arrived from British North Borneo with a letter addressed to Bill Presswood. It was from an Australian officer, requesting Ernie to visit North Borneo. The officer promised, "I will send a number of soldiers for an escort if you will come, as it is not safe to travel alone." But we had received our orders to go no further.

The officer also asked if one of our national teachers could stay with him and preach to the Dyaks. Those Dyaks, he said, were very difficult to manage because of their enslavement to rice liquor. He added, "Your Dyaks are different."

That statement was true. Many Dyaks had changed. They had accepted Jesus the Son of God as their personal Savior and the Holy Spirit had worked in their hearts. They were not merely reformed, but had become new creations in Christ Jesus.

Many years later, the English author J.C. Pollock reported that Ernie was called "Tuan Change" among the Murut Dyaks of British North Borneo, because, they said, so many of their lives had been changed by following Christ. Although Ernie had never been to British North Borneo, the good news had been carried there by the Dyaks whom Ernie had discipled years before. (See "Appendix II.")

Many activities were planned for our last Sunday in Long Berang. People were rejoicing. Confessions had been made. Broken fellowships had been mended. Of particular note was the fact that there was peace between those who had taken up arms against the Japanese and those who believed taking up arms was wrong. That was a major victory. All had gone to bed in peace that last Saturday night.

At about 4:30 a.m. the next morning, a piercing gun shot awakened us. The scream of a woman and the crying of a child followed. Ernie jumped up, grabbed the flashlight and ran toward the river. I stood shaking like a leaf, reminding myself of the verse in the Psalms, "What time I am afraid, I will trust." I knew it was better to "trust and not be afraid," but this time I was afraid. The only thing to do was to trust and keep on trusting.

Within a few moments, Ernie returned to the house with a smile on his face.

"What happened?" I asked, still shaking.

"A Dyak policeman shot off a gun," Ernie replied.

"But why?" I pressed.

"To wake up the people for the sunrise service!"

That was not what I would have chosen as a wake-up call, but I agreed with Ernie that it had worked. Even before the sun peeked over the mountain, the whole village was awake.

It was a beautiful, never-to-be-forgotten day. The Christian Dyaks gathered outside the Mission house where long logs had been arranged for seats to protect us from the heavy dew. They insisted that I use a chair which they placed in the midst of the logs.

What a special gathering it was! People dressed in all kinds of outfits filled the log benches. Some were well covered, others barely covered at all. Some were outfitted in Army clothes, looking quite professional. The earnestness on their faces was inspiring. Their shining white teeth marked them as Christians—no black stains from chewing betel nut. Nor were their cheeks bulging or their lips stained red, drooling and spitting red saliva everywhere.

In front of the logs was a bench with a board in front of it to kneel on. A chair served as a table for the communion elements: the bread, the emblem of Christ's body broken for us and for the Dyaks; and the wine, the emblem of Christ's blood shed for us and for the Dyaks.

Ernie administered the sacraments as the 200 or so worshipers marched forward row by row, kneeled and partook of the bread and wine. All was quiet and reverent. How far-reaching God's love had been! God was here with His people in the jungles of Borneo! And we were there because Jesus had given us a commandment: "Go ye therefore, and teach all nations, baptizing them in the name of the Father, and of the Son, and of the Holy Ghost: teaching them to observe all things whatsoever I have commanded you: and, lo, I am with you always, even unto the end of the world" (Matthew 28:19–20).

What a privilege! What an honor! The experience was overwhelming. I praised God for each missionary who had lived with, witnessed to and taught these people. Ernie had made the first trip to this district in 1932. "As far as I know," he had written then, "there is not one person here who knows what it means to be saved."

The communion service was followed by a baptismal service down at the river. Nine Dyaks followed the Lord in baptism and then the memorable conference was over and most of the people dispersed to their villages.

That night, in the silence of the tropical night, Ernie and I sat on the steps of the house talking about all that had happened—the good things and the bad. We realized there was much to be thankful for, but there was also much left to pray about.

Ernie asked, "Would you like to come back here and work among these Dyaks?"

With only a slight hesitation, I said, "Yes. Yes, I would."

The hesitation was triggered by my awareness of the isolation, the hardships, the dangers. Could I endure a steady diet of this and be a good soldier of the cross? Certainly not in my own strength. There was already one grave on a little hill behind the Mission house: the grave of Laura Harmon Presswood, Ernie's first wife. They had been married only two years before she went to be with the Lord.

Also, I knew that Ernie's heart was with the

they would have the gospel of Jesus Christ. He felt very much at home with them.

Ernie continued.

"Ruthie," he said tenderly, "I don't know why you have had to go through so much in your first term on the mission field. Most missionaries in their whole lifetime don't go through what you have in less than five years."

I knew there was no answer to the why. One thing I did know, however—I had never planned on having an easy time.

In the midst of our conversation, Ernie suddenly asked, "What would you do if something happened to me?"

Stunned, I clapped my hands to my head.

"My dear, I don't know!" I answered haltingly.

He continued, very seriously.

"I would like you to go home to the States . . . and in time, marry again. I love you . . . I want you to be cared for . . . I want you to be happy."

As he paused briefly I tried to corral my racing thoughts. *Was I hearing right? Was he serious?*

Then he went on jokingly.

"Ruthie and Jimmie—that sounds nice!" He was teasing me about a Jimmie back in New York.

Our talk was abruptly ended by a frontal attack of a host of gnats and mosquitos. We retired into the one screened room of the house. We needed a good night's sleep. Tomorrow, once again, we would be headed back downstream.

The night did not turn out as we hoped. We both spent a restless night—I with a frightening dream and Ernie unable to sleep. I awoke in the middle of the night. Ernie wasn't beside me.

Groping in the darkness I finally found him in the bathroom at the end of the long hall. He was feeling sick and had diarrhea. We both knew that meant trouble.

"We must get out of here," he said.

I knew enough not to question him at such a time. There was little sleep for either of us in the few hours that remained.

Early the next morning Ernie met with the Dyaks who were going to take us downstream. They said the river was too high to travel. But we could not afford to delay, as another conference in the Bulongan district had been scheduled for the end of the month.

Ernie decided that we should leave everything possible in Long Berang in the way of clothes and food because the people were in such need.

"But," he added, "don't leave that blouse you made out of the two dish towels. That looks cute on you!"

16

The Rapids

*"And let them sacrifice the sacrifices of
thanksgiving, and declare his works with
rejoicing." (Psalm 107:22)*

The following day, January 16th, the river had
receded considerably. We could be on our
way.

We shook hands and said goodbye to the folks at
Long Berang. As usual, this took longer than expected. The long, narrow boat was packed to
capacity with rice and personal belongings. One
Dyak was taking a pig to the coast to sell. Three of
the seven boatmen were headmen, a situation
which made for stimulating interpersonal dynamics.
Usually a long canoe had only one headman, but all
three were eager to take us downstream on our
journey.

Ernie and I stepped into the boat and headed for
the center seat in the widest part of the boat.
Someone gave us a couple stalks of sugar cane for
when we got thirsty. As we paddled away from the
shore and out into the main stream, someone
yelled, "The birds are flying the wrong way to travel

today!" However, for some reason the Dyaks determined to go anyway.

Although all was going well for a short distance, I soon began to worry about shooting the rapids. Looking to Ernie for encouragement, I asked, "Whatever happens, happens quickly, doesn't it?"

He answered, "Yes."

Not having received too much comfort from that reply, the only consolation I had came from knowing that the Lord answers prayer quickly, too!

In a short time, I was experiencing first-hand the thrill of shooting the rapids. It was fun! It reminded me of the toboggan slide in Chestnut Hill near Buffalo. As we approached each rapid, the boatmen headed for the swiftest part where the water met from the two sides. I hung on for all I was worth.

At one of the largest rapids, we climbed out of the boat. The foaming waves were high, dashing against boulders and hidden rocks. We crawled along the river bank, grabbing limb after limb, always looking for a spot big enough to put a foot. The rocky walls and sod were wet and very slippery.

I was totally unprepared for what happened next. Leeches and more leeches attacked me all over my body—I estimate between 50 and 70 of them. We were trespassing on their home, the wet leaves and vines on the side of the riverbank.

I was dressed in summer clothing—a thin dress, undergarments, straw hat and sneakers. I felt their injections as the leeches fastened onto my skin and began to suck out my blood. The day before I had read in an Australian Army book what to do about leeches. They recommended touching them with a burning match or a lighted cigarette. All well and good—I had neither one!

In the meantime, the Dyaks had portaged the baggage over the rapid. They fought skillfully, wrestling the boat through the angry waters.

Finally, we came to a spot where we could climb back into the boat. I tried to get rid of the leeches, but the more I touched them the deeper they bored into my flesh. I had to let them fill up with blood before they would drop off. By then, they were about the size of my little finger. Ernie and the Dyaks tried to help, but to no avail.

"My dear," Ernie observed, "this is the first time I've ever seen you excited!"

"Well, this is something to be excited about," I retorted somewhat sharply. The leeches felt like snakes wrapped around my body, but finally satiated, they eventually dropped off of their own accord.

We continued shooting the rapids for several more hours. Then came the big one.

The Dyaks got out and anchored the boat. They climbed a mountainous boulder jutting out into the river. The big question was whether we should stay in the boat or get out and pick our way along the bank again.

After much discussion, a boatman came back and announced, "We are staying in the boat." It would be difficult, they said, to find a place to anchor the boat on the other side of the rapid so that we could get back in. That was fine with me. At that point I was convinced that leeches were worse than rapids.

We drifted out into the stream and passed the enormous boulder that obstructed our view. Once in the flow, however, we realized almost immediately how impossible it was going to be to travel through this rapid.

The first big wave, about 10 feet high, half filled the dugout with water. With the onslaught of the second one, we were all tossed into the churning tide.

Ernie grabbed me around the waist and we clung together as the current carried us swiftly downstream, tossing and turning us like clothes in a washing machine.

The boat went over our heads. We bumped into rocks. Though we sank down and down, we didn't touch bottom. In about 300 yards we came up for air only once. For a while my straw hat helped me stay near the surface, but then the rubber band under my chin broke and I lost the hat.

The next thing I knew, a Dyak was grabbing my hair. I felt a chunk rip out of my head. It didn't hurt, perhaps because the water was ice cold. I was encouraged to know that they were trying to rescue us. Thoughts of death flashed through my mind. I was sure it was all over.

Finally, another man grabbed my arm. When my head surfaced again, I had my right arm tightly around Ernie's neck. The Dyak holding my other arm was balanced precariously near the stern of the overturned boat.

He struggled to pull us onto it. He would have been more successful had he not been holding his pig in one arm while pulling me from the water with the other! We finally managed to pull ourselves up onto the bottom of the boat while it continued to ride the current downstream.

We were able to get ourselves into a straddle position and at that point I was glad that the boat wasn't any wider! One thing we had accomplished—we were through the rapids!

We rode another 100 yards or so, straddling the bottom of the boat. As we came close to a rock near shore, someone yelled, "Jump!" We obeyed almost automatically and swam to the rock.

In short order the Dyaks had the canoe in its proper position. Fortunately, it was not much the worse for the ordeal—only one board had to be repaired.

We had left Long Berang at 7 a.m. It was now about 1 p.m. and we were only about half way to Malinau, our destination.

Our food had gone to the bottom of the river along with the rest of our baggage. My sneakers had been pulled off my feet. My dress was so torn that only part of the skirt remained. Ernie had lost one of his heavy Army boots. But we had survived! What a miracle!

John Willfinger's tin trunk had ridden the rapids, lodged under the seat of the dugout with the lid partly open. There, among the papers that had fallen out onto the canoe floor, a birthday card caught my eye. In bold print it read, "It's a crime to forget a fellow's birthday!" It made me wince. Today was Ernie's 38th birthday and I had forgotten all about it!

Safely back in the canoe, we glided along

smoothly in the now peaceful river. A dugout similar to ours appeared in the distance. As we met, the canoe pulled to the side under overhanging branches. A young Dyak boy with a broad grin on his face stood up in the boat.

"Dawat!" exclaimed Ernie. "What a wonderful surprise!"

Dawat was the Christian Dyak boy who had stayed with us in Makassar before the war. He had rescued our roll of blankets and mosquito nets as they floated down the river and had wrapped them in a rubber Army sheet. Dawat was headed for Long Berang, where he planned to visit his mother and then return to Makassar Bible School. We had a short visit and then said goodbye, looking forward to seeing him again soon.

Later that evening, finally back at Malinau, we stayed once more at the rest home. Everything we owned was either gone or else was soggy, wet and torn. We had had nothing to eat since early morning. It was too late to get much help, but Ernie managed to find a Chinese family he had known previously. They gave us a small bowl of rice and a promise of more food the next day.

While Ernie put up our salvaged mosquito net, I collapsed on the desk top, utterly exhausted. That night, we slept in our torn wet clothes on wet blankets covered with a rubber Army sheet.

The next morning dawned and, thankfully, the Chinese family did show up to help us. The wife gave me one of her own dresses to wear. Ernie found an old board and carved a pair of *klombs* for each of us, similar to the ones we wore in the internment camp. He made the leather straps out of the one Army boot that the rapids had not claimed.

With the necessities of life more or less taken care of, Ernie tried to obtain transportation to Tarakan. Two days passed. We were beginning to wonder how much longer we could hold out with no food, no money—nothing with which to sustain life.

That evening, the Chinese man who had helped us with food and clothing came for a visit. As the evening progressed, Ernie asked him, "Have you ever heard the way of salvation that God has provided for every person who will believe and accept it?"

The Chinese man said he had not.

As Ernie related the story of Jesus in English to the Chinese man, it came to my heart as more beautiful than ever.

That was why we were there—to tell the story of Jesus and His love.

Finally, a government motor boat came to pick up some soldiers and prisoners. They expected to leave early the next morning for Tarakan. We made plans to be on that boat, too, even though they didn't want us.

17

A Promise Kept

"Fight the good fight of faith, lay hold on eternal life, whereunto thou art also called, and hast professed a good profession before many witnesses." (1 Timothy 6:12)

The next morning at 3 a.m., in a desperate attempt to leave Malinau, we went down to the motor boat before it was loaded. The vessel, called a duck, was an amphibian common during the war.

We found ourselves a seat perched high on a long board next to the driver. The soldiers then herded the 30 prisoners into the lower well. We were in the awkward position of having to stare at them, and they at us, for the whole trip.

Included with the prisoners were 25 men accused of murdering Dutch civilians at the time of the Japanese invasion. This very eventful day, beginning in the wee hours of the morning, would last into the wee hours of the next morning.

Some distance down the Sesayap River, we anchored at a village. A number of soldiers left the boat and lined up single file with their bayonets extended. They were, we were told, going into the village to capture at least one man who was a murderer. They warned us that there might be shooting. When they returned, over an hour later, several more were added to the already grossly overcrowded boat.

A little further down the river we stopped at another village. This time the soldiers confiscated goods that had been sold on the black market.

By the middle of the afternoon, with all the heat and excitement and no food, I had come to the end of my strength physically, mentally and emotionally. I could hardly sit up any longer. I looked at Ernie in desperation. He was suffering, too. Quietly he started quoting from Psalm 107:1–8:

> *O give thanks unto the LORD, for he is good: for his mercy endureth for ever.*
>
> *Let the redeemed of the LORD say so, whom he hath redeemed from the hand of the enemy;*
>
> *And gathered them out of the lands, from the east, and from the west, from the north, and from the south.*
>
> *They wandered in the wilderness in a solitary way; they found no city to dwell in.*
>
> *Hungry and thirsty, their soul fainted in them.*
>
> *Then they cried unto the LORD in their trouble, and he delivered them out of their distresses.*
>
> *And he led them forth by the right way, that they might go to a city of habitation.*
>
> *Oh that men would praise the LORD for his goodness, and for his wonderful works to the*

children of men!

As Ernie quoted the Scripture, the powers of darkness seemed to be lifted from me. I received a wonderful healing touch that I could not explain except as the gift of a loving Heavenly Father.

By the time we reached the Celebes Sea, a portion of which had to be crossed to reach the small island of Tarakan, night had fallen once again. All around us was black as ink. The harbors had been mined, making it very important to be in the right place, following the right directions.

We almost reached Tarakan at one point, but had to go back out to sea again because we had entered the wrong channel. The only light the boatman had to steer the craft with was a flashlight. The second time, we chose the right channel and finally reached Tarakan Island safely.

The trip we had taken into the interior of Borneo—to Long Berang—had taken about four months to complete. Ernie was thoroughly exhausted, but he immediately began making plans for the trip to Tanjungselor. When we were there in December, Ernie had made arrangements for the Christian workers from the interior to gather at the coast for a conference at the end of January. It was now past the middle of January.

Before Ernie left, we had a couple of days together—just long enough to replace the clothes and shoes we had lost in the rapids. Ernie was outfitted with Army clothes again.

My clothes were more difficult to replace because women's clothes were scarce. We visited a

Chinese *toko* (store) that had some yard goods. For my birthday, January 22nd, Ernie purchased enough material for three dresses. What more could a girl want! Another wonderful surprise was that I finally received the first letter from my mother in over four and a half years!

Before the Australians had pulled out, a padre had ordered a pair of nurses' black military shoes for me. They arrived within a few days. Once I became accustomed to the tightness of shoes again, I found them very comfortable.

On January 30, 1946, Ernie left very early in the morning for Tanjungselor. It was always an ordeal to say goodbye, but this time the parting seemed more difficult than ever.

"I will be back in five days," he promised. Ernie was a man of his word. I knew that if it were humanly possible, he would be back in five days as he said.

That afternoon I went for a walk with a woman named Satoni. She was the wife of John Willfinger's cook, Jahja, in Long Berang before John gave himself up to the Japanese during the war. Satoni was not a Christian and her behavior was questionable in a number of ways. She and I hadn't gotten very far from the guest house until I felt I had to go back.

"Are you sick?" Satoni asked.

"I'm all right," I replied. I felt weary. I just needed a good night's sleep on a comfortable camp cot with a warm blanket.

I tossed and turned all night with a high fever. The next day, Dr. Jasin, a Javanese doctor from the Netherlands Indies Civilian Administration hospital, called on me. He ordered a nurse to stay with me in our nine by 12 foot room which contained two camp cots, a small table and a chair.

I became so weak that I was no longer able to drink from a cup, so the Muslim nurse gave me a sterling silver, long stemmed spoon to drink through. The spoon seemed out of place in those surroundings.

Speaking with difficulty, I requested the nurse to read from my Indonesian New Testament. She picked up the book and walked to the table where the coconut oil lamp was flickering. I waited and waited for her to read aloud, but all was silent except for the strange night sounds. No words came from her lips, though she appeared to be reading.

I tried again to make my wishes known.

"Please read anywhere in the book so that I can hear." The silence continued. Oh, how I longed to hear the Word of God for encouragement and strength!

Seemingly unable to get the nurse to read to me, my mind turned to the chorus " 'Tis So Sweet to Trust in Jesus":

> Jesus, Jesus, how I trust Him,
> How I've proved Him o'er and o'er;
> Jesus, Jesus, precious Jesus!
> Oh, for grace to trust Him more.

Did this Muslim nurse read in a way that her soul would be enlightened to know Jesus? I never knew, because in the morning I was moved to the military hospital and never saw her again.

The military hospital was a crude one room quonset hut about 30 by 60 feet, which boasted only a dirt floor. There were two long rows of bamboo beds, all of them full. I was quarantined in the corner of the room by two reed walls and two bedsheet walls.

The doctor looked for symptoms of typhoid fever, since it had been two weeks since we had upset in the Sesayap River. Typhoid was a possibility, but I insisted I would be all right in five days. I had had alarming fevers before.

My life seemed to be hanging in the balance. My mind went in and out of delirium. I had visions of an altar of burning hot coals falling through a grate down to ashes. I felt as if I would be leaving this world.

At one point, I turned my head toward the wall. As I did so, the Scripture from Second Kings 20 flashed through my mind. Hezekiah, too, had turned his face to the wall in desperation and cried out to the Lord. God had added 15 years to Hezekiah's life. At that very time, when I, too, was crying out to the Lord, I believed He would add 15 years to my life.

I heard everything that was taking place on the other side of my walls. Some things alarmed me. Someone had given a patient an overdose of hypodermic medication. The patient lived, but only "by the skin of her teeth."

On the other side of my reed wall, a young Chinese boy had died. A carpenter was called in to make the coffin. The father and others of the family stood by while the coffin was sawed and hammered shut. The carpenter had a double challenge because the father kept throwing himself across the coffin, weeping and wailing for his son.

Several Indonesian girls took care of me with tenderness and love. I guessed that most of them had had very limited nurses' training, but when I was too weak to lift a finger, I appreciated all their ministrations.

Three of the nurses brought me gifts. The first gave me a well-worn blue handkerchief. The second gave me a well-worn pink handkerchief. Insignificant though these gifts now seem to be, it was almost unheard of to own a handkerchief during war time in Borneo. Another girl gave me several things, something different every day—a bar of soap, a toothbrush, and the like. One time she gave me a pair of pillow slips.

A day or so later, I heard someone being reprimanded for stealing. Pillow slips were specifically mentioned. Putting all the information together, I realized that the nurse must have stolen the things she gave me. She may have been dismissed then and there, because I never saw her again.

When I was on my feet again, I went to Dr. Jasin and told him about the gifts, especially the pillow slips. I wanted to return them. Dr. Jasin, however, refused to accept the articles and told me to keep them. It had been several years since I had used a pillow, to say nothing of a pillow slip.

Each day new people came into my life who were "friends indeed" because I was certainly in need. I believe my Heavenly Father sent those people to help me.

Among them were three Christian workers who had attended the conference in Tanjungselor. I managed to gather together enough strength to ask whether Tuan Presswood was all right. They answered in typical Indonesian fashion "Ada baik—baik saja" (Is good, good only). They did say that he had been sick. The real truth was that they had come for me because Ernie was acutely ill. Seeing my own condition, they had decided not to tell me.

Finally, February 3rd arrived, the day when Ernie planned to return to Tarakan. I had looked forward to this day of promise, the day we would be together again and perhaps begin a life that could be called normal.

We could begin our marriage once more. We could be together in ministry. We could pursue the plans that we had begun to formulate from the time we first knew that God was placing us together to serve Him. Maybe we would even go back to Long Berang. These pleasant thoughts spurred me on to get better.

I kept praying that the Lord would give me strength. My fever had left in five days, just as I had predicted, but what days of suffering they had been. Now, I was gaining strength, but very slowly. I could even take a few steps.

I insisted on going back to our room at the guest house so as to be there when Ernie arrived. This was to be the first day of the rest of our lives and I wanted to be there to start it right! Dr. Jasin consented to let me return by ambulance only if I would promise to take complete rest.

I had no sooner got settled in my room when Mr. and Mrs. Van de Berg, the Dutch controller and his wife, came to see me. I thought it was a social call since they, too, had been interned at Kampili Camp.

But, no. They bore the news that everyone already knew except me!

Ernie had come back the day he said he would, but only his body. He had become acutely ill in Tanjungselor and had gone to be with the Lord two days earlier on February 1, 1946.

I could not believe it! I remember saying, "No, not my Ernie! Not my husband!" I felt faint and thought I would pass out. Mrs. Van de Berg held a glass of something to my lips, urging me, "Drink this; it will help you."

I took one sip and pushed it away.

"I don't need that," I said. It was some kind of alcoholic beverage.

Mrs. Van de Berg made another attempt to help.

"We will pray for Ernie," she offered. That statement brought me to my senses.

"Oh no, you don't need to pray for Ernie," I responded. "He is all right. He is with Jesus. Pray for me!"

I later learned that Ernie had become sick with headache, chills and fever almost as soon as he had arrived at Bulongan. After the first day, he was too sick to carry on the ministry, but insisted that the conference go on. Sunday afternoon, the national teachers and deacons met in his room for communion. Ernie shook hands with them all and gave them advice and instructions.

Four days later, as his temperature soared even

higher, Ernie began to be concerned about his condition. His attendants wanted to come for me but Ernie said no, that I was not strong enough to endure the trip.

On February 1st, Ernie was able to eat a little and he was encouraged. He told the men the story about our upset in the rapids and asked Guru Tondok to pray for us. After a few minutes he said, "I do not want to talk anymore. I want to be quiet and see what is going to happen to me."

Later in the afternoon, Ernie once more called Guru Tondok to his side.

"Brother," he said, "I am very tired and cannot stand it any longer. By appearances, I must go up and that is far better. I just found out and now I understand. It is all right. Brother, I will go and enter a place that is good. Brother, don't forget your work! To backslide is bad! Yes, we must go ahead! Go ahead, and don't be afraid. Brother, I must go. The work is on your shoulders. I won't be able to go to Makassar, but there is nothing I can do about it. . . . All right, Brother, I am so tired. Feel I must go. Tell my wife so that she will be all right. Brother, I want to go!"

About 5 p.m., Ernie took Guru Tondok's hand and said, "Thank you very much." His face was shining and his eyes were bright. He went to sleep again.

About 9 p.m., Ernie asked to be raised up and then to be put back down again. When the men saw that he was breathing his last, they joined in prayer and committed him into the Lord's hands. When they opened their eyes, he was gone.

The trip to Tarakan with Ernie's body had been extremely difficult and dangerous. Guru Tondok and several other men had started across the bay from Tanjungselor to Tarakan, a trip which usually took one and a half days. But the small motorboat had given out and they were forced to return and find new transportation.

Finally, the Sultan of Tanjungselor loaned the men his own motorboat. After the second try, they were able to reach Tarakan. Ernie had, even in the most difficult of circumstances, arrived home the day he said he would.

The funeral was held that very day, as Ernie had been dead for three days. Three days before burial in the tropics is a long time. They would not let me see him or attend the memorial service, which was conducted by the Dutch officials.

He was honored with a 21-gun salute. I heard the shots as I lay on my camp cot in the room we had shared. The customary native music and drums sounded far into the night to appease the evil spirits.

It was another seven days before I regained my strength. I spent the long hours on the camp cot searching the Scriptures, looking for promises in God's Word that would encourage me and increase my faith. But the promises I read seemed to be ones that Ernie and I had claimed together.

Then, from the depths of my soul, I found myself crying out: Why was Ernie taken from me? I'm so alone in this place. Who can I trust or not trust? How much power do the evil spirits have over the people? Or for that matter, how much power do the evil spirits have over me? Terrible darkness threatened to engulf my soul.

I didn't know what to do. There had always been other missionaries around. *What would Ernie do?* I wondered. Problems had to be solved and decisions had to be made. I felt forsaken, so alone. And what about our furlough, already one year overdue, which we were planning to take in May?

Finally, about two weeks later, a breakthrough came. I was reading Psalm 107:22: "And let them sacrifice the sacrifices of thanksgiving, and declare His works with rejoicing." My sorrow, it seemed, must become a sacrifice of praise, a sacrifice of joy.

Although such a sacrifice seemed more than I could bear at that moment, a glimpse of light began to pierce the darkness. But a terrific battle still lay ahead, for it was one thing to read and to give consent to such a thing, but quite another thing to do it.

I realized that Ernie's will was not to be the ultimate word, but God's will. He was the One whom I served.

Long, lonely days followed, but the Lord once again impressed the familiar verses on my mind and heart: "I can do all things through Christ which strengtheneth me" (Philippians 4:13); and "That the trial of your faith, being much more precious than of gold that perisheth, though it be tried with fire, might be found unto praise and honour and glory at the appearing of Jesus Christ" (1 Peter 1:7).

Several weeks had passed since the body of John Willfinger had been exhumed and reburied in the

European cemetery. Ernie had conducted the memorial service. Now Ernie had been laid to rest beside John. The real memorial to these two soldiers of the cross was the church of Jesus Christ established in the heart of East Borneo.

No previous experiences in my life shocked and devastated me like Ernie's death. Life took on a feeling of unreality. Surely at some point in time Ernie would return. Night after night I heard his footsteps coming down the hall.

But slowly, I had to realize the awful truth that Ernie had come home for the last time. He had lived a whole lifetime in just 38 years. He had come to the end of his Borneo trail.

We had been so happy to be together again out of the internment camps. Praise and prayer had been spontaneous. Now, I couldn't pray no matter how hard I tried. Bewildered, I just existed from one day to the next. People were kind. They expressed sincere sympathy. But at the same time, they avoided me because they didn't know what to say or do.

The day after the funeral, Guru Tondok, who had cared for Ernie during his last days and who accompanied the body to Tarakan, came and offered to become a mediator between me and the outside world. I had very little money. I didn't know how to barter and trade, so Guru Tondok took care of that for me. He was kind and gentle and soft-spoken—truly an angel from the Lord in my time of perplexity and crisis.

One day, a young Dutchman with whom we had become acquainted appeared at my door. We exchanged greetings and then he said, "I brought back my wife. I want you to meet her."

"That would be nice," I replied.

"Where's your husband?" he asked.

My mouth opened. But no words came.

Finally I blurted out, "He died."

The expression on the man's face remains imprinted on my mind to this day. He was visibly stunned. But it was also a moment of revelation for me. Ernie was dead. It was time to turn my thoughts to my future. What did God want of me now?

I had come ready to serve Him, to lay down my life for Him if necessary. Although death could easily have happened at many points in the years just passed, God had preserved my life. What the future held, I did not know.

One thing I did know, however, was that my life was still in His hands. His will was my will. I was willing to live for Him and even die for Him. At times the latter would have been easier. But as Dr. Jaffray had said, "You will not find it so easy to die."

18

Goodbye to Borneo

"My heart is fixed, O God, my heart is fixed:
I will sing and give praise." (Psalm 57:7)

As I was trying to address my own state of affairs, 11 Dyak boys came downstream from the Sesayap District. Ernie had made arrangements to take them with him to enter Makassar Bible School. Now, Guru Tondok assumed responsibility for the boys, most of whom had never been to the coast before.

The question soon arose of what to do with the clothes Ernie had acquired from the Australians. That problem was solved when a couple of the Dyak boys exchanged rice for the clothes. Abai, the chief spokesman for them, bought Ernie's shoes even though they were several sizes too big.

My decision regarding the Dyaks was to get them to Makassar, where the Dutch government, thanks to the intervention of a certain Captain Jezeer, had promised to supply them with food. Getting them there was the next challenge. Travel was hazardous at best. Once again, Captain Jezeer's help was invaluable, for everything was risky, except where the

Lord intervened. (Captain Jezeer had written me a
letter of condolence after Ernie's death.):

> The short interval I learned to know him
> leaves me with an admiration for his fervent
> activity and unsurpassing faith in his mis-
> sion. Always, I will remember him as the
> first man who came to this area without a
> weapon and with the only purpose of bring-
> ing the real and only peace back to human
> hearts, as soon as the terrible struggle and
> bloodshed in this area had ended.

Finally, on March 6, 1946, one month and six
days after Ernie went to be with the Lord, a ship
was to set sail from Tarakan to Balikpapan. That
would be at least halfway to our destination. We
seized the opportunity to go. The Dyaks were especially elated that the day had finally come when we
could be on our way.

At Balikpapan we were transported to an airport
about 20 miles away, where we boarded a B29
bomber that would take us to Makassar. I did not
know at the time that one just like it had dropped
the atom bomb on Hiroshima and Nagasaki.

As we approached the plane to load up, the pilot
appeared. He looked different from any pilot I had
ever seen. He had a sweat band tied around his
head. The sweat band made his blond hair stand
straight up and blow in the wind. Excitedly waving
his arms, he exclaimed to me, "If any airmen in the
United States would see the storm we are taking
off in, they would say we were crazy."

Despite the ominous prediction, we all climbed into the plane. The trip was rough and stormy, with the plane riding like a roller coaster, dropping and then soaring again. My stomach rose in my throat and once again fear began to grip my heart.

I noticed a mother holding her four or five-month-old baby in her arms. The baby was sound asleep. At that moment the Lord spoke to me: *You can trust Me just like that little baby is trusting his mother.* Peace flooded my heart.

The B29 landed safely in Makassar on March 20, 1946. My gang dispersed to various places—the Dyak boys to the Makassar Bible School, Guru Tondok and others to their homes and various destinations.

Once again I found myself back at the Lajan-giroweg Mission address. Rev. and Mrs. Walter Post were carrying on bravely, in spite of the difficulties of the nine months since peace had been declared. No recruits had come from America. There was much political unrest. Some national workers, with insufficient funds to carry on, sought work or ministry elsewhere. It was a frustrating time for all concerned.

About 100 letters had arrived for Ernie and me while we were away those four months. What an encouragement they were! It took me three weeks to read and answer the letters from Ernie's friends, many of whom I had never met. But among them was at least one name I knew—Minnie and Jimmie Hutchins. Ernie had told me what a great blessing they had been to him through the years. They had even sent supplies for the house he had built in Long Berang.

Ernie and I had planned to leave for America in April or May. Now I found myself faced with going home alone. Fear began to rear its ugly head. I was afraid to stay and afraid to go. I knew that sooner or later I would have to face the world, especially family members and friends at home. With all the failures and setbacks I had experienced, the enemy of my soul tore at my feelings of self-worth.

Nevertheless, the time came when I realized it was best for me to return home. I did not want to add another burden to the Mission.

Mr. Post made arrangements with the New York board, who requested that I also take Philoma Seely to America. As a result of both mental and physical torture at the hands of the Japanese secret police, she would need a lot of assistance in getting home safely.

Mr. Post tried to find us a passage by ship, as planes were not flying in or out of Makassar at this time. The plan was to get us to Singapore where more contacts could be made for the rest of the trip to America.

Over a month went by before we found out about a U.S. liberty ship heading to Singapore with a load of oil. Through the kindness of the captain, we were able to leave Makassar on the U.S. Thomas Bradley. Other ships, with their all-male crews, had not wanted to take the chance of allowing two women on board.

A major requirement for us was to get a doctor's permit saying that we were physically fit to travel. An officer from the ship tried to cut through some of the red tape for us, even to accompanying me to the clinic to make sure the permit was worded correctly. I knew the man only as a Mr. Smith from New Jersey.

Fortunately, Dr. Goedbloed, the lady doctor who had taken care of me in the internment camp, was on duty. She made sure that both Philoma and I had a satisfactory doctor's permit.

Packing didn't take long. Philoma had one suitcase and I had one that had been left in Makassar by another missionary. I also acquired a small Army trunk in which I packed some of John Willfinger's belongings—his Bible, some snap shots, a fountain pen with his name engraved. I planned to pass them on to his mother.

I also packed some things for Margaret Jaffray that had belonged to her mother and father. My two *parangs* (long knives) from Borneo were in the trunk, along with a few other souvenirs. The *parangs* were especially valuable to me. Ernie had bargained for them: "I want my wife to have a *tanda mata* (an eye remembrance or keepsake)." When Ernie tried a second time, on another occasion, the owner refused to sell it. After Ernie died, the owner, in a gesture of sympathy, sent it to me.

Several wedding gifts, which had meant much to Ernie and me at one time, were left behind for use by the Mission workers. Among them were the sewing machine, typewriter, chiming mantel clock and many books that had been salvaged, including a set of *Encyclopedia Britannica*.

About one hour before we were to leave the Mission house for the ship, Mrs. Post rushed into my

room to say that one of the national workers
wanted to see me.

I walked into the living room and saw Mel sitting
on the edge of the chair. He had something rolled
up in his lap. We exchanged greetings.

"Mrs. Presswood," Mel proceeded hesitantly, "I
have Mr. Presswood's suit. It was stored in an oil
can. During the war, when I was married, I needed
a suit. I had this one made to fit me."

The suit in his hand was the navy suit Ernie had
worn at our wedding!

"Mrs. Presswood, will you please forgive me for
taking it? Do you want it back?"

"Of course, I forgive you, Mel," I replied. "You
may have the suit. I am glad someone can use it."

We shook hands and said farewell.

Thus began the dreaded goodbyes—to Vi and
Walter Post, who had watched over me and lent a
helping hand in every way possible, to the friends I
had made over the past five years, friends from the
Bible school, especially the Dyaks, the people from
the tabernacle and the national workers.

Many watched and waved as Philoma and I got
into the car and drove away to the harbor.

19

America the Beautiful!

"In all thy ways acknowledge him, and he shall direct thy paths." (Proverbs 3:6)

Up to this time Philoma had been quite cooperative, but as time went on, she became less agreeable. I loved her because of her friendship in the past and in the most difficult times tried to concentrate on the real Philoma, the one I used to know.

My thoughts went back to the Kampili Internment Camp and the time I was acutely ill with possible pneumonia. Philoma had sought the Lord in my behalf, praying through the night into the early morning hours. Now, I wanted to help her in whatever way I could.

Before actually reaching Singapore, we arrived at the tip of the Malaysian peninsula and dropped anchor. Another vessel shuttled us into the city. So many ships and submarines had been sunk in Singapore harbor and surrounding areas that sailing ships were not allowed to enter. Also, the waters continued to be mined.

The captain kindly contacted the Methodist Girls' Mission and found them willing to give Philoma and me temporary lodging. A smiling lady named Miss Sader welcomed us and showed us a place to sleep on a long porch.

Miss Sader and I, we soon found out, had many things in common. She, too, had been interned by the Japanese, but in Singapore. She, too, would soon be going home on furlough.

We had been informed that in a couple of days a troop transport would be sailing for the United States via Manila. That meant we would have to take care of all arrangements without delay if we hoped to be on that boat.

Meanwhile, our expenses mounted. Paying for taxis and lodging had depleted my resources. I contacted our Mission headquarters in New York City, giving them a report of the journey so far. They wired me $150 in American money (two weeks' pay). When I went to claim it at the bank, the clerk refused to give me anything but Singapore money. Back at the Methodist Home, I told Miss Sader about my problem.

"I can get American money," she assured me. "I will exchange it for you."

The next day I had to get a passport photograph, make legal arrangements and contact the shipping company for traveling requirements. This time, Miss Sader offered to watch Philoma for me and gave me a young Chinese girl named Wee to accompany me around the city.

Wee and I started out in the morning to take care

of the errands. All went well until we reached the shipping office where we had to make arrangements with the officials of the Marine Fox Troop Transport.

It was already late afternoon. We were told to be seated and took our place with about 20 others also seeking transportation to America.

During the long wait we struck up a conversation with an American lady named Mrs. Lim. She had been married to a Chinese man. Now she hoped to return to the United States with her two children, a boy, 10, and a girl, 18.

It was getting very late and we still had not had our turn at the wicket. We knew that in Singapore, "nice" people, and especially women, were not on the streets or in public places at this time of night. The telephone rang in the office. It was Miss Sader.

"Are you all right?" she asked.

I assured her that we were, but that I didn't know just when we would return.

When I hung up, Mrs. Lim asked, "Do you have a ride home?"

I shook my head.

"Would you ladies like to ride with me? I don't think you will be able to get a taxi at this hour. My chauffeur is waiting for me."

What else was there for us to do? Whatever we did, we were taking a risk.

"Yes, we would appreciate the ride very much."

Mrs. Lim continued with the plans. "I know where the Mission home is. We will let you off at the bottom of the stairs on the street below. You can walk up the stairs to the street where the home is located." This sounded feasible to me and Wee didn't object.

Finally, at 11 p.m., after five hours of waiting, my name was called and arrangements were made for Philoma and me to get to America.

Wee and I climbed into Mrs. Lim's limousine for the offered ride. When we arrived at the stairs, Wee and I jumped out of the car, expressed our thanks and said goodnight. We locked arms and started up the 150 stairs that rose beside a hotel up to the next street. By the time we reached the top, we were tired and out of breath.

"The Mission is the second house," Wee commented.

The distance to the first house I guessed to be about one block. There were fields on both sides and no street lights.

Up ahead I noticed a man walking toward us on the same side of the street. I suggested to Wee that we cross over to the other side. When we crossed over, the man did, too. We were both praying. As he came closer, a short desperate prayer escaped my lips, "Jesus, help us!" We clung to each other.

Suddenly, the man, in a British Indian uniform, complete with badges, grabbed me. In obscene English he left no doubt of his intentions.

Wee pulled on me, desperately trying to free me from the vice-like grip of my assailant. She managed to yank one of his arms loose and I ducked under the other one. I was free!

Then the man grabbed Wee. She let out such a blood-curdling scream into the stillness of the night that he let her go. All the time we were edging toward the houses. I grabbed Wee's hand again and we ran as fast as we could to the Mission house.

In response to our banging, Miss Sader opened the door and drew us in. We had had no food since morning. Over tea we rehearsed the experiences of the last hours. It had been quite a day—and quite a night!

But there was no time to dwell on the past, for it was already after midnight and we were supposed to be down at the dock at 3 a.m. I tried to call a taxi. There was no response. For a while it looked impossible for us to get to the troop transport in time for the sailing.

Although it was such a late hour, Miss Sader called a Methodist minister who lived on the other side of the city and asked him if he would transport us to the dock. He kindly agreed. We paid him $10, but his assistance was worth much more.

As we were being driven through the eerie streets of Singapore, Philoma was quiet. That was a relief.

We were among the first ones to arrive at the dock and we moved about cautiously. Philoma and I sat down on our baggage and waited for the motorboat ride to the U.S. Marine Fox anchored outside the harbor. We felt, and probably looked, like two forlorn little waifs.

When we finally boarded the ship, we were shown to a large room with many bunks. Many other young women, most of them war brides from India, would share the same room with us.

As a group of them began to voice disparaging remarks about our country and our American boys,

my Canadian/American blood was fast coming to
the boiling point. When I could stand it no longer,
I stood up, identified myself, and stated, "I am an
American and I love my country." Why were the
girls going to America if they considered it such a
bad place, I wanted to know. I ended my speech
with a veiled threat: "You could be put off this ship
if the captain knew you talked like this."

I truly thought that was a distinct possibility, but
instead, guess who was put off the ship at Manila?
Philoma and I, along with the rest of the civilian
group that had boarded at Singapore. The majority
of the women, we found out, were the wives of
American officers!

Once again we were stranded, but at least I had
been in the Philippines. I wasn't prepared for what
I saw in the once-beautiful city of Manila. It was a
complete disaster.

Since Philoma and I were still under the wing of
the United States Army, we were taken to an Army
base. It would become our home for the next nine
days. The accommodations were considerably improved, as we were assigned to one of the few
buildings of the Santo Tomás University that still
remained after the war.

I felt encouraged and thankful. I was beginning
to see a pattern of God's leading in all the difficult
places. The Lord had posted someone in each spot
to watch over and help us along the way. In fact, I
began to look for the people God was sending our
way. It became an exciting adventure.

It had been over five years since the time I had
landed in Manila as a new missionary and had

stayed for one month with the Baptist missionary women. At that time I was waiting for my visa to enter Netherlands East Indies. Ernie had gone on ahead to Borneo so that he could be back in the country before his one-year re-entry permit expired.

As I remembered it, the Santo Tomás University was located just a few blocks from the Mission house. In the earlier days I had often walked around the university because its grounds were adorned with beautiful flowers and palm trees. I also recalled that the address of the Baptist Mission was 401 Pennsylvania Avenue.

In hopes of finding someone I knew, I went for a walk around the area. It was bleak and bare—no buildings or houses, no big trees to protect me from the burning sun. I came to a street sign that read "Pennsylvania Avenue." In the distance was a small white building surrounded by barren land. Sure enough, the number 401 was on the corner of the building. The Baptist Mission had survived the war!

The building had several rooms, including a chapel and a reading room. GI's had helped rebuild it after the war and many of them were still there enjoying Christian fellowship and serving in many different ways.

I had often heard about clothing and other things coming from missionary barrels. Now, I was about to learn the full significance of a missionary barrel. The ladies at the Mission were very kind and invited me to select something from their own barrels. I picked out a dress, a pair of pajamas and a bath towel—God's gifts from the loving hearts of His people.

One day, an officer's wife came into the army barracks where Philoma and I were staying.

"I have just arrived from the States to be with my husband," she said. "My things are not through customs yet. Would you by any chance have a towel I could use? I would like to take a shower."

I showed her my towel and told her she was welcome to use it. It was the towel from the Mission barrel.

When I returned to my room sometime later, I found it rolled up at the foot of my bed with a thank-you note and an American dollar bill inside. Again, the Lord had posted His special helper for me.

I had to make the now familiar rounds to fulfill all the official regulations. The American Consul was at the Army Replacement Center in Quezon City, almost 20 miles outside of Manila. Usually I could leave Philoma with someone when I went on errands, but this time I had to take her with me.

We got on a bus that we hoped was headed in the right direction. Finally, we arrived at the Army base, which was actually a settlement of tents which provided military offices and accommodations for former prisoners of war who were en route to the United States and other places.

A distinguished-looking man walked by me. He looked very familiar because of his well-trimmed goatee. Suddenly, I realized that it was Rev. Konemann, a Dutch missionary under The Christian and Missionary Alliance in Netherlands East Indies. I had never met Mr. Konemann personally, but I recognized him from pictures.

I introduced myself and learned that he and his wife and three children had come from Java where they, too, had been interned by the Japanese during the war. They were also waiting for transportation to the United States.

My job was to find the office where we could obtain passage to the United States. Philoma and I continued walking until we found the large tent where such official business was transacted.

We were interviewed first by Captain Glenn. I saw immediately that he had been a war victim because he had only one arm. Next, we talked with Sergeant Greer, whose desk/table was at the end of the tent. Both men were kind and understanding, especially when they learned of our circumstances.

The next interviewer was the American Consul, a Mr. Joslyn (if I recall correctly). He asked many questions and I answered for both of us as best I could.

"I told you people to get out of there before the war," he scolded. "You should have gotten out of there." He was clearly irritated.

I kept quiet, as a lengthy explanation did not seem appropriate.

In conclusion he said, "You will have to report to my office in Manila."

At this point, Captain Glenn spoke up and said, "Sir, it would be difficult for them with all the extra traveling under these circumstances."

"If they can come out here," the consul retorted, "they can come to my office in the city."

Philoma and I left the tent and headed out to the road to catch a bus back to Manila. We hadn't gone far down the dirt path when I heard someone call my name. I turned around to Captain Glenn's friendly smile. He told us he was from Kansas, Philoma's home state.

"Will you please accept this?" he asked, extending an open hand. "I'm sure you can use it."

He handed me 20 pesos (about $10 in American currency). I thanked him sincerely.

"You are very welcome," he responded. "We want to help you. We'll see that you get to the U.S. Marine Jumper with your baggage."

What a relief! *Thank you, dear Heavenly Father.* Another angel planted by God! We arrived back at our lodging place tired, but glad to have a good bed to sleep on.

As instructed, Philoma and I made the trip to downtown Manila and met with the consul. Why we had so much trouble over our papers, I never did learn. Philoma was an American citizen traveling with no passport, but I had been able to preserve my passport through the war.

After nine days of being detained in Manila, we were finally cleared to continue our journey. Captain Glenn and Sergeant Greer picked us up, as promised, and drove us to the harbor. I never saw them again, but they were God's helpers for two needy missionaries.

On June 29th, we boarded the U.S. Marine Jumper, a large troop transport. At last, we were homeward bound!

Each passenger had to find his or her own niche for the trip. I had an upper bunk and Philoma had a lower one. Most of the people around us had been interned in Manila during the war. Many had physical and/or mental problems.

For two days we had smooth sailing, but it was short-lived. A storm blew up and increased in strength as time went on. How well I remember the last evening meal we were able to attend. The rain was beating against the ship. There was the sound of howling wind, thunder and lightning.

Very few people dined that night. Most of the food was dumped overboard by the barrelful. What a sickening sight! Not many months before we had been in internment camp on starvation rations.

The next day was no better. We were in a raging typhoon. All the women in our room were sick. Oh, how sick we were! The ship's crew passed out oranges for us to suck on. That was all we had to eat for about three days.

The vessel continued to heave and roll. First, we would go down, down, until it seemed as if we would reach the ocean floor. Then we would start upwards, going higher and higher until the rudder would shimmy and shake the whole ship. The gyrations continued for a couple of days. Because of the storm, the captain decided to forego a planned stop in Japan. Instead, we went straight out to sea, taking a more northern route across the Pacific Ocean.

Nearing the west coast of America, we headed due south toward San Francisco. It was night when we passed under the Golden Gate and into San Francisco Bay.

America the beautiful! I never expected to see it again.

20

"Ruthie and Jimmie"

*"O magnify the LORD with me, and let us exalt
his name together." (Psalm 34:3)*

Because of our schedule change, we arrived in
San Francisco one day early. Philoma and I
were almost the last ones to walk down the
gangplank.

Everyone around us was greeting friends, taking
taxis, packing into cars, making telephone calls.
They all seemed to know where they were going
and what they were doing—except me.

I looked over the crowd. There were no familiar
faces. Once again I was alone.

I began to panic. Everything was so fast-paced. I
had returned to a very different culture from that
of the Indies. I did not know anyone in the city.

Then I remembered that in my address book was
the telephone number we had used six years earlier
on our way to the Netherlands East Indies. Yes,
the little book had survived the war. I still have it
today.

I searched for a telephone, but couldn't find one.
Under the sign "Travel Bureau" sat a stately woman

in a uniform. She appeared to be helping people. Since I had not used a telephone for almost six years, I wasn't sure I knew how.

Explaining why we were there, I asked the woman if she would call the number for me. When the party answered, she handed me the phone and once more I explained who I was and why I was calling.

The voice on the other end said, "Oh, we thought you would be coming tomorrow! We will be right down to pick you up." That was encouraging.

I called headquarters at New York and reported where we were. They requested that I take Philoma to her family in Winfield, Kansas, as soon as possible.

My next telephone call was to my mother in Albion, New York. What a joy to hear her voice! Dad and my eight brothers were comparatively well, she said. Avery had arrived home from France. Bob was home from Germany. Keith would soon be coming home from Guam. Dean was stationed in Denver and had signed on with the ground Air Force. Gerald had served on land and was not required to do foreign duty. The older boys, Byron, Harold and Pete were not drafted because of their age. There was so much to talk about, but we decided to save it until we were face to face.

Philoma and I stayed in San Francisco for a couple of days. The Alliance Christians helped me make the travel arrangements by train to Kansas. It was a wonderful relief to place Philoma into the hands of her loved ones. She had endured untold suffering. I hoped that life would hold more joy and peace for her in the future.

I purchased my ticket for Buffalo, New York, via Chicago and sat down to wait for the train. I had a while before it was time to board so, having gained a bit of confidence in telephone calling, I decided to let my mother know my arrival time in Buffalo.

A few minutes later, as I sat on the bench with nothing to do but wait, I checked my purse for my ticket. It was gone!

In a panic, I went to the ticket agent and explained my predicament. The ticket agent had me write my name, address, occupation, etc., on a form. As he watched me write, using a fingernail-sharpened pencil, he exclaimed, "Now, no missionary here has to write with a pencil like that!" He gave me a new pencil, nicely sharpened. Then he proceeded to help me with the ticket search.

"Empty everything out of your handbag to make sure the ticket isn't in it," he advised. *He must know about women's handbags,* I mused. Mine was a big one which had been Lilian Marsh's before the war.

I emptied out everything. No ticket.

When I finished, he ordered, "All right, now backtrack everything you did."

I hadn't moved around very much, but had made that call to my mother. I looked in and around the telephone booth, but saw nothing. Then I slid the door back and forth. There, behind the door, was the white envelope with the ticket in it! Once again God had someone in the right place at the right time for me.

Later that day, July 25, 1946, I arrived in Buffalo. I was home!

Mother and Dad tried lovingly to get me through those difficult first days. Mother sent me to the beauty parlor at the first opportunity. My hair was very thin and a variety of lengths—some had been pulled out in the rapids and some had fallen out because of the high fevers. I tried not to comb it very much, because each time more hair came out.

What clothes I had were worn and badly out of date, so my family took me shopping. Dad took my borrowed suitcase to the repair shop to get it mended. The buckle had collapsed and by the time I got home, it was being held together with a rope. Nearly every day Dad bought me ice cream and all kinds of food that he thought I would like.

One time, in the middle of the night, I was sick to my stomach. Mother came into the bathroom.

"Ruth," she said tenderly, "can I help you?" I realized then that I was indeed home with people who loved me. It brought unspeakable release to my soul.

I was examined by the New York Board of Physicians. As a result of their report, The Christian and Missionary Alliance officials granted me six months without any responsibilities.

I appreciated their gesture, but, now that I had reached home alone and had started a new chapter in my life, I found that I dreaded facing not only people, but the future. People seemed to expect so much of me (and rightly so), but I felt weak, disappointed and depressed.

With all my heart I wanted to be strong and courageous in the Lord. Instead, doubts and fears gripped me. I wanted to forget the experiences I had had, but they returned night and day to haunt and torment me.

Medical help was available for most of my physical problems—tooth decay, lingering amoebic dysentery, gastro-intestinal complaints and back ailments. Later on, however, I would need five abdominal operations over a period of eight years.

I found myself going deeper and deeper into depression and, before I knew it, the six months had almost passed. The inevitable return to work was fast approaching. I was to serve with a Bible and missionary conference in Canada, which started about the first of March. I did not feel prepared—physically, spiritually or mentally—as hard as I tried to be nor as much as I wanted to be.

Some things I clung to—God had not changed, His promises had not changed, Jesus my Savior had not changed. It was I who had changed.

Day and night I pleaded with God to make me what I ought to be for His honor and glory. I asked Him to forgive me for my sins of commission and omission, for wrong attitudes, for lack of love for all souls, for lack of faith. Also, I needed to be forgiven for the sin of pride, because I did not want anyone to know what dire need I was in. I saw my righteousness as filthy rags, but I clung to the promise, "I will never leave thee nor forsake thee," and with the Psalmist, I declared, "My heart is fixed, Oh God, my heart is fixed; I will sing and give praise."

With my thoughts tumbling over one another like barrels in whitewater rapids, I got the conviction that I must pull myself together for the spring mis-

sionary tour. I needed to go by faith in what the
Lord would do for me, because I was not able in
my own strength.

Billy Sunday once said, "Some people, instead of
trying to drown their troubles, take them out and
give them swimming lessons." That was my personal diagnosis of my condition.

In fear and trembling I went to Toronto, Canada,
about 140 miles away. I spent several days with
Ernie's mother and father and a few cherished moments with Lillian and Violet, Ernie's twin sisters.
Both were married and had families.

The day of the first meeting of the conference arrived. We (Miss Gladys Clark from Colombia, Rev.
G.C. Ferry and Rev. Jean Funè from French In-
dochina) rode most of the day from Toronto to a
small church in Chatham, Ontario. Rev. Nathan
Bailey, the district superintendent, escorted us
throughout the whole tour, speaking at each service along with the missionaries. (Dr. Bailey later
became the president of The Christian and Missionary Alliance.)

The extensive traveling, sleeping in different beds
and speaking each night finally took its toll about
the third conference. I felt I couldn't go on. My
head was sore to touch and it was painful to comb
my hair. A tension headache made me nauseated
and gave me such pain in the back of my neck that I
was forced to stay in bed. I missed an evening service. But the Christians prayed and God answered.
That was the only meeting I missed on the whole
tour.

A similar situation arose some days later. This

time I was to speak to about 50 children and a few adults. I had been fighting a headache all day. As I walked into the auditorium, I could see the enthusiastic faces of the children as they crowded into the front seats.

I sat down on the platform and prayed, "Dear Lord, help me; I don't think I can make it."

I spoke for a few minutes and then showed my slides of Borneo. As I did so, the headache left me. The rest of the trip was headache free.

The six-week tour ended near Toronto, where I had the privilege of having dinner and spending a pleasant evening with the Baileys and their two young daughters, Joyce and Carol. I felt much better at the end of the tour than at the beginning. All praise to God!

I was scheduled to speak at the Delta Lake Camp near Rome, New York. It had been about one and a half years since Ernie and I had talked about going home together on furlough. At that time he remarked, "One of the first things we will do is attend a camp and have our souls fed."

In the middle of the conference week, I went forward when an altar call was given. It was then I confessed for the first time the burden of fear in my heart that I would not be able either physically or emotionally to take the rigors of life on the mission field.

I was prayed for and anointed. I do not remember what the counselor said, but I do remember what happened to me: warm, soothing oil poured over my whole being inside and out. One thing I knew—wherever life placed me, I would trust Jesus

Christ my Savior and serve in whatever capacity I could. I longed for complete healing of mind and body.

The burden had lifted. I felt free. I knew that there was a future for me, but what, I did not know.

My next assignment was at the Summit Grove Camp in the beautiful rolling hills of the picturesque farm lands of Pennsylvania. Summit Grove had been an old Methodist campground. By the time the Alliance bought the property, it was 100 years old and looked its age!

The round tabernacle, with straw on the floor and long hard benches, stood in the middle of the camp, surrounded by other buildings. At the front of the tabernacle, above the altar, were bouquets of fresh gladioli. The flowers were grown and arranged by one little lady as a service for the Lord.

Around the tabernacle in a wider and wider circle stood quaint cottages and two-story duplexes. Each house had a small veranda across the front and a lean-to kitchen on the back. Often the veranda had a rocking chair on it. The cottages had never been painted.

One afternoon as I stood near the tabernacle, a man with a shiny clean face came up to me, smiling. I say "shiny clean" because his bald head, white shirt and the sun's rays made him look that way.

He introduced himself as James Hutchins of Chester, Pennyslvania. James Hutchins. Something clicked in the recesses of my mind. I knew that name! This was the Jimmie Hutchins with a wife named Minnie who had been such faithful friends of Ernie and Laura through the years. This was the man who had bought and sent supplies to Borneo for the house at Long Berang.

As we talked, we discovered there had been many changes in our lives.

Ernie had died February 1, 1946. Jimmie's wife, Minnie, had died the same year in May. Jimmie had been left with three children—Doris, 17, Helen, 15, and Charles, 13.

Before the week ended, we had become quite well acquainted. My fall tour would take me through Pennsylvania, Maryland and Washington, D.C. The last church on the tour would be the Hutchins' church in Chester, Pennsylvania.

Jimmie and I saw each other several times during the next few weeks. He would often come and take me from one appointment to another.

The tour eventually ended and I returned home to Albion, New York. My friendship with Jimmie, however, did not end. It grew into love and a desire to be committed to one another. We became engaged in November, 1947.

"Ruthie and Jimmie." Ernie had said it first that last day in Long Berang as we had talked about the future. Had he known something then that I did not know?

When Jimmie asked me to marry him, one of his comments was, "I do not know what it is to be unhappily married."

I replied, "I don't either."

Marriage meant many changes in my life including becoming a mother of three children. I welcomed the challenge. To me, the children were an added blessing, as I feared I would not bear a child of my own.

One and half years later, however, I gave birth to a baby girl. We named her Martha Jean.

God gave Jimmie and me 31 years together, years that were filled with the happiness and struggles that most families encounter. At age 72, on March 3, 1978, Jimmie went to be with the Lord. Martha Jean and her husband, Larry, and their two children, Stephanie and Jimmy, opened their home to me—another gracious gift from the hand of my loving Heavenly Father.

I have been blessed. Our sovereign God planned all things well, even when I did not understand that the trials of my faith, though often painful and unwelcome, would eventually prove to be more precious than gold.

> *"Wherein ye greatly rejoice, though now for a season, if need be, ye are in heaviness through manifold temptations:*
>
> *That the trial of your faith, being much more precious than of gold that perisheth, though it be tried with fire, might be found unto praise and honour and glory at the appearing of Jesus Christ." (1 Peter 1:6–7)*

Epilogue

At the time of this publication (1993), Ruth Presswood Hutchins is 82 years old and lives in Columbus, Ohio, with her daughter, Martha Jean, and her family. One of her ministries at the First Alliance Church, where she is a member, is the oversight of the church's 3,500-book library.

Ruth also likes to read, work with water and acrylic paints and write letters—especially to Indonesian missionaries.

The Hutchins' son, Charles, and his family live in New Jersey, and daughters, Helen Heisler and Doris Gaska with their families in Pennsylvania.

Ruth has two grandchildren, eight step-grandchildren, and six great step-grandchildren.

Philoma Seely returned to Indonesia in 1950 under another Mission. She died four years later at Balikpapan, Indonesia.

Lilian Marsh spent a total of 40 years (nine in China and 31 in Indonesia) in missionary service. She returned to the field in 1949 and died January 31, 1964, of a stroke in Bandung where she is buried.

Although badly beaten during her seven weeks in prison, *Margaret Kemp* returned to Indonesia and worked together with Lilian Marsh. She died

June 29, 1968, of a heart attack and is buried in Endicott, New York.

Darlene Deibler married Jerry Rose and returned to New Guinea where she lived for nearly 30 years before beginning a new ministry at a remote ranching settlement in the Australian outback. Her story is chronicled in *Evidence Not Seen*, published by Harper & Row, San Francisco, copyright 1988. Permission to quote from her book is gratefully acknowledged.

Mrs. R.A. (Minnie) Jaffray and Margaret returned to Canada soon after they were released from internment camp. The strain of those years had left Mrs. Jaffray weaker in body than either she or others realized. Following an extensive trip to visit friends in various parts of the United States and Canada, Mrs. Jaffray passed suddenly into the presence of the Lord on November 10, 1946, at the age of 75. Her missionary service had spanned 52 years.

Margaret Jaffray, following a furlough and the death of her mother, returned to Indonesia in 1948. However, because of ill health, she came home to Canada just two years later. Margaret passed away July 25, 1959, from injuries sustained in an automobile accident near Orillia, Ontario, Canada. She was 52 years old.

Appendix I

This article was written by P.J. Luijendijk in Dutch and given to Ruth Presswood in Makassar. It was printed in the Alliance Witness *(now* Alliance Life*), June 29, 1946. Used by permission.*

God Selects the Best

Note: The following interesting account of some of our brethren in the Japanese internment camp in the Netherlands East Indies was written by a missionary of one of the Dutch societies and translated by Mr. M.M. Lourens. It gives us the best glimpse yet afforded of the life and fellowship of that difficult period.

"But when the fruit is brought forth,
immediately he putteth in the sickle,
because the harvest is come." (Mark 4:29)

The sad news of the sudden demise of Mr. Presswood, one of our best friends in the internment camp, brings again to our mind the many blessings received through him and other missionaries of The Christian and Missionary Alliance in the years which now lie behind us.

After the occupation of the Netherlands East Indies by the Japanese in the beginning of 1942, all European citizens of the great East were interned, and the camps originally spread over the various islands were brought successively to South Celebes and united into two large camps, one for women and children and one for the men.

Our camp for men grew gradually to about 600 persons, among whom were 35 missionaries from all corners of the Great East; an extraordinary reunion, but rich in blessing! The Sumba group, to which I belonged, arrived in July, 1942, at Makassar. There, very early, I became acquainted with Messrs. Deibler and Presswood. (Mr. Jaffray had not yet been interned.) They lived together, and it was a pleasure to make their acquaintance—Mr. Deibler always genial and kind to everyone; Mr. Presswood, sober, simple, reserved; less approachable than Deibler, but with a heart of gold.

We Netherlands missionaries were in the beginning foreigners to them, and they to us. We had heard much about one another, even too much. They were representatives of the English-speaking world, of another theological and ecclesiastical point of view, of another way of living. But their kindness and sincerity compelled us to a continued acquaintance. We soon discovered that we were near together because we loved the same Saviour. The closer we came to Him, the better we understood one another. I remember the first sermon by Mr. Presswood. We, as Protestants, had united services, alternately in Dutch and English. His text was Hebrews 6:1, "Let us go on unto perfection."

His method of text exegesis was different than we were used to in the Netherlands, but the contents of his message moved me. Internment had caused a crisis in my life of faith, and he drove me forward to all that Christ has prepared for us, a depth far above our expectations.

At the end of September, 1941, our camp was transferred from Makassar to Pare-Pare, 150 kilometers (about 93 miles) to the north. There we occupied a military post. Presswood and Deibler lived together in section 5. Everyone who visited them was heartily welcomed. Already in Makassar, they had begun holding Bible conferences in which, alternately, they took as their subjects the great biblical figures. Many have followed these courses with great interest and blessing.

Christmas, 1941, brought, besides Protestant and Roman Catholic religious services, a Christmas celebration for the whole camp. Deibler was one of the speakers. He was a very good speaker; it was a joy to see him and to listen to him. That evening he told us the legend of the "Fourth Wise Man" from the East, who found his Saviour hanging on the Cross.

Deibler was an enthusiastic propagandist. In various evenings he told me about the organization of The Christian and Missionary Alliance—of its founding as a "faith mission," of its work in the most isolated regions, among peoples not yet touched, of its active prayer for the speedy return of Christ, about the training of the missionaries (which I would like to have had, too), of the important place of prayer in the prayer meetings at home and on the mission field. This last touched me the most. I must honestly confess that prayer had never occupied a large place in my life and work. Deibler told me of his work in Borneo and near the Wissel Lakes in New Guinea, and how he lived with his native teachers, to be able to pray with them often.

New Year's morning 1943, Deibler spoke on James 4:14: "For what is your life? It is even a vapour, that appeareth for a little time, and then vanisheth away." It was his last New Year's morning! Who could have thought it! Some time later he spoke on John 21:1–14: "Cast the net on the right side of the ship."

In the spring of 1943, Mr. Jaffray, with some others, was brought into our camp. It was sad that Japanese would intern a person of such an advanced age. Mr. Jaffray was given a small room in the hospital in order that he might be better cared for, and very soon he was able to walk, when it was favorable weather, with Mr. Presswood or Mr. Deibler. We became only superficially acquainted with him, but Presswood and Deibler spoke always with great respect of him and his work. He was a noted laborer in God's kingdom.

The death of Deibler came very unexpectedly to him and to all of us. He was ill only a few days; and many and sincere prayers were offered for his recovery, but God willed otherwise. Presswood told me later, "I had prayed fervently for him, but toward midnight the Lord convinced me that I should no longer do so. Then I surrendered him to our Saviour." A few hours later he departed from us, to heaven, the first of the three friends. He was beloved by all.

In March, 1943, still a fourth American missionary from Ambon entered our camp, Mr. Whetzel. He was in many respects of the same spirit as Deibler and Presswood, lived later together with Presswood, and certainly was a great help and consolation to him after the loss of Deibler. In the middle of 1943 we became attached to Presswood in a very special manner.

We decided to gather together every day between Ascension and Pentecost to pray that we, too, would be completely filled with the Holy Spirit. Presswood and Deibler had informed us about such prayer meetings, which are unknown in Holland in general. Our desire, however, was so great for deepening, that we laid our plan before Presswood, and asked him to take part in our conferences and to show us the way. This he did, and for that I am most grateful to him. God used him in such a way that he became a blessing to us all. In us, he found difficult pupils; we did not surrender easily, having to gain the victory over many objections (mostly of dogmatical and psychological nature). But God has taken hold of us, and has kept us together, and has made us understand in the course of two years the deeper meaning of prayer. Not that we have now learned everything—certainly not—but we have been given the direction, and we have experienced that prayer must and can be a living reality, the real meeting place with our Father in Christ Jesus. We thank God that for that He gave us Presswood. These prayer meetings became later a blessing to a large group within the camp.

After the arrival of a group of twenty English-speaking persons from the Christmas Islands, it became necessary to hold a religious service in English every Sunday. Previously Anglican services had been held for a group of Armenians in our camp. A heavy task was thus laid on the shoulders of the English leaders: Messrs. Presswood, Whetzel, Woodward and Snaith (the last two of the Salvation Army).

In the meantime, Presswood earnestly prepared himself for his task after the war. He made further study of the Malay language and tried to obtain as complete information as possible about every mission field from which a missionary was present in the camp. Through such knowledge and through his personal connections, he could have become after the war an excellent link between The Christian and Missionary Alliance and the Netherlands Protestant Missions in Indonesia.

Toward the end of October, 1944, we were bombed out of our camp by the allies (by mistake). In great haste, our camp was transferred by the Japanese to a valley about five miles from Pare-Pare, where some pig sties without walls became our abode. On account of the bad hygienic condition, an epidemic of heavy dysentery broke out which struck down two-thirds of the camp and claimed 25 victims in a short time. Mr. Presswood, too, was sick for a long time, emaciated considerably, and looked very pale. Fortunately he recovered later.

Mr. Jaffray and about 15 other men were housed in the so-called "Old Men's House," back in the valley, in a shadowed spot near a spring. Here they were safe from danger from the sky. Often I have seen Messrs. Presswood and Jaffray sitting there together. In these difficult circumstances, Mr. Jaffray really bore up splendidly.

The allies approached nearer and nearer. The bombardments along the west coast of Celebes became all the time heavier and more frequent. In April, 1945, the allies landed on Tarakan. That was the reason why the Japanese carried us, head over heels, in trucks, into the interior for about 156 miles deep into the mountains to a place 50 kilometers (about 31 miles) beyond the last administrative post (end of May, 1945). It was a terrible trip; pigs were transported in a more decent manner than we were then. It is a miracle that older men like Mr. Jaffray survived this, but many of them were broken through it. We were placed in a deep valley, at an altitude of 1,300 meters (nearly 4,300 feet)—always misty and rainy, while we had almost no clothes left. The rations became steadily smaller and poorer; it became a "hunger camp."

Soon Mr. Jaffray was brought into the hospital, completely exhausted. We tried to give him some extra food, whatever there was, though there was really nothing that would bring relief to so aged a man in such circumstances. First it appeared as if he would recover, his energy and humor returned, but it was only for a few days. Then he was led by Jesus tenderly to the eternal home of the Father.

Presswood had cared for him as for his own

father, and I believe that he lost in him a good father. On the Sunday after his death, Presswood held a memorial service on the hill, near the little cemetery, where he described the work and the person of Mr. Jaffray in detail.

Peace came to us completely unexpected. The receipt of news was very scarce, especially in the last camp. We were returned from the hunger camp, Bolong, to Pare-Pare and from there to Makassar. Suddenly the enemy became much more polite. Soon thereafter the Australians landed in Makassar and took control. The families were united after a separation of three years, and all of us were furnished with some house facilities. How Presswood enjoyed all of this! Also the reunion with his congregation at Makassar. Finally—back again: the long awaited moment! And now—full speed ahead with the work!

In November Mr. Presswood departed for Borneo, his last voyage. We thought that he stood at the beginning of a new, beautiful period of work. How often had he prayed to be free again, to be able to work for Christ! With great love he could pray for blessing on the native churches here. But the Lord our God willed it otherwise.

We have received much from these men. They were living witnesses for Christ. And when the fruit was fully ripe, God put the sickle therein, because it was the time of the harvest.

Human beings forget one another in so short a time. The vacant places are immediately occupied by others. But for the children of God there is an eternal home. They are not forgotten, neither they nor their works. They receive the complete companionship, after which they have strained during their lives with prayerful longing, and their desires have been gratified. May all of us, also the sadly bereaved families of our brethren, be consoled with that, and may it encourage them to follow our Good Shepherd loyally.

We shall have to continue our missionary work here without these three brethren. Without them, but yet—as I hope—in a new, a stronger, closer relationship. No matter from which people or church we come, we missionaries need one another here so very badly. There are differences; but if we acknowledge the same Christ, the Son of God, as our Saviour, then there is more that unites us than divides us. We have still so much to learn, one from another. We have lived together, and we have been able to pray together. May true cooperation between us be the good fruit of this bitter time of internment.

Appendix II

The following article is taken from the World Vision Magazine, *1968, pp. 22–25. John Pollock later included this in his book,* On Fire for God, *copyright 1990, John Pollock. Published by Marshall Pickering, an imprint of Harper Collins Publishers Ltd., London. Used by Permission.*

Tuan Change
by John Pollock

On the Sarawak coast in East Malaysia, a missionary tapped excitedly at her typewriter as she compiled an information sheet datelined 1968: "Reports have been coming through of a great stirring among the churches of Indonesian Borneo. . . . Several Christians have had visions from the Lord which they have been told to proclaim to their people, and as a result, hundreds have repented from sin and turned to the Lord. The spiritual stirring is influencing Murut and Kelabit churches on the Sarawak border."

She glanced across the airstrip to the Bible school. They were just clearing up after the half yearly conference which 200 indigenous pastors and leaders had attended. Some had walked eight days through the jungle, others had come by mission plane or river boat. They represented an expanding, missionary-hearted church of many tribes in the mountains and jungles of former British Borneo.

It all went back to the pioneering of one forgotten North American, William Ernest Presswood, who, because he died young a few months after the end of World War II and lies buried in Borneo, has been largely forgotten except by those who loved him. But his name is legendary among the natives of the interior: They call him "Tuan Change"—because so many were changed from a particularly evil darkness into the light of Christ.

Ernie Presswood was born on the prairies of Canada in 1908, son of English immigrants. In a Sunday school class which could boast of 11 who later became ministers or missionaries, he gave his heart to Christ. Yet it was not until the Presswoods returned to England briefly in the early 1920s, and he heard Gypsy Smith, that he dedicated himself for service. Back in Canada his father bought a meat and grocery store in Toronto and Ernie trained as a motor mechanic.

After attending Prairie Bible Institute in Alberta and Nyack Missionary Training Institute in New York, he joined The Christian and Missionary Alliance and went to the Netherlands East Indies in 1930.

About 18 months later a most extraordinary rumor passed round among the Murut or Dyak natives far up country in the interior. As it was told to me in Borneo long after, from a Murut named Panai Raub, "We were clearing the undergrowth for the new season's farming when we heard of a wonderful white man they called Tuan Change, because he changed wicked natives and said they could have a new life. He was on an island off the coast." They wanted to go down, but were afraid of venturing where Malays, Chinese and whites lived.

His Middle Name Was "Hurry"

The Muruts, a large tribe scattered across the mountains of the British Dutch border, were steeped in spirit-worship to such an extent that planting would be endlessly delayed for lack of an omen, or the half-grown paddy abandoned by another. They turned most of the harvest into intoxicating rice beer, sapped their tribal stamina by sexual malpractices, and frequently went headhunting. They lived naked except for loincloths. "When I heard," Panai Raub continued, "away up in the hills in the midst of all that drinking and fear of the spirits, about change and new life, I just could not sleep for desire. Two months later, when we were felling the big timber, we heard that Tuan Change was downstream. We all went to meet him, taking our sick."

They found Presswood at Long Berang, a place above fearsome rapids which needed considerable courage for a lone westerner to negotiate, even with skilled boatmen. A huge crowd of Muruts, heads bowed, squatted around Presswood who was standing with eyes closed, arms outstretched to the sky.

"What is this?" thought Panai Raub, "What are they doing?"

After praying, Tuan Change unfolded some pictures and preached in Malay with one of the few educated Muruts interpreting.

Panai Raub was right in front. "I could hear every word. Some of the others could not. He preached on the Resurrection, with amazing effect on the crowd. Right from the beginning it hit me. I was just drinking it in. When I first heard the Word, I believed."

This was in September 1932. Next day Tuan Change left them and walked far over rugged jungle trails in intense heat until forced back to the coast with a foot ulcerated by leech bites. He wrote home: "What a time I have had. Physically it has been a hard one, but the results have been *glorious*. I think around 600 Dyaks were reached with the message."

Ernie Presswood was now nearly 25. He was a true pioneer, willing to forego the good things he enjoyed. He pushed himself relentlessly.

"His middle name could have been 'Hurry,' " writes one who knew him well. "He was always praying, reading, teaching, counseling, studying, with a little notebook always at hand."

He seemed austere, not quick to laugh, though with a genuine sense of humor. He was a perfectionist. Hiding the compassion which ran strong within him, he could be hard on those who had openly acknowledged Christ, yet failed Him. His was a character that could be appreciated and admired by the Muruts, who seemed so weak and ineffectual then, yet subsequently disclosed the same characteristics of uncompromising dedication.

Bad Foot Limits Work

Presswood was kept at the coast by his bad foot until 1934 when he paid a second visit to Long Berang. "I have been here two weeks, twice as long as I expected, the interest has been so great. From early morning till late at night I have been kept busy with scarcely a break. Pray much for me, for the strain is very great. Thus far I have baptized 130, and I expect there will be at least twice as many more."

After a third, longer visit he returned to America and married Laura Harmon from Pennsylvania. In May 1937, they settled in Long Berang, after taking 29 days to negotiate the rapids.

That Christmas there was a great baptism at Long Berang. One of those baptized was Panai Raub. The following April Presswood could write of a "morning service at which the Spirit of God was manifest in a very real way. Waves of praise swept over us as we looked into the faces of these happy Christians."

A few days later, when the Presswoods were still the only whites upriver, Laura had a miscarriage. Complications developed. There was nothing Ernie could do but see her die. He buried her in a coffin made with his own hands from one of the timbers with which they were building their home. Despite sorrowing natives he felt desperately alone. "Only those who have passed through such a heartbreaking experience can appreciate the distress."

Then floods swept down on Long Berang, carrying away much of their precious timber. Ernie wrote, "Surely the Lord doesn't love me when He treats me thus, I thought, but He answered me so blessedly, 'Whom the Lord loveth He chasteneth and scourgeth every son whom He receiveth. . . .' The comfort and blessing that He has already sent upon my soul have strengthened me and given me courage to face the future."

For Borneo, it was already proving a great future, for the revival was spreading right across the border. The Sarawak Muruts had been even worse than the Indonesian. Officials of Rajah Brooke, the English ruler, estimated the whole community except the dogs to be drunk a hundred days a year. After Tuan Change's first visit to Long Berang, rumors of his good words filtered over the border and some Sarawak Muruts went to find an Australian missionary, Hudson Southwell, who returned with them in 1933. Several were converted, but Rajah Brooke reckoned the Muruts irredeemable. He refused Southwell permission to settle, threw a *cordon sanitaire* around the whole tribe and left it to die out.

Panai Raub and other baptized Muruts determined to evangelize their cousins. Presswood had not told them they should. He so preached Christ that converts caught the vision for themselves. Long before it became accepted missionary strategy, Presswood urged that a church should be self-propagating and self-supporting.

"I Do Not Drink Now"

"The first village I came to," Panai Raub says, "just over the border, a big drinking party was on. I refused it: 'I do not drink now.' 'Why not?' 'Because I follow the Lord Jesus Christ.' 'Where did you hear about Him?' 'From Tuan Change' 'Does he live near this Lord Jesus?' They were very pleased and keen to hear. Even the old people who had been heavily involved in headhunting and the old worship brought the fetishes and burned them."

Panai Raub was not yet literate and no Scriptures had been translated. He preached with the aid of pictures. On his next visit he found that drinking had been abandoned. Wherever he went "there was not one house among the Muruts which did not want to hear, 'Eternal life.' That's what we want, they would say." After he left, a village would choose its own church leaders from those who showed the gifts of the Spirit.

White Man Doesn't Meet Standards

Late in 1938 the Rajah of Sarawak heard that something extraordinary had occurred. He ordered an expedition of inquiry, led by a government official and a missionary. They traveled among the Muruts from December 12, 1938, to February 4, 1939. The government official reported that he was not popular with the Muruts because he smoked, drank whiskey and did not possess a Sankey hymnbook! After that, missionaries of the Borneo Evangelical Mission were allowed to settle.

Meanwhile, across the border, Presswood undertook even more rigorous climbs to reach mountain villages. By the time he left for his second furlough late in 1939, the Murut church was growing rapidly.

In America he was married again, to Ruth Brooks of Buffalo, New York, who returned with him in May 1940. He was appointed to head the Bible school at Makassar in the Island of Celebes. Here the Japanese invasion engulfed him. Beaten, starved, forced to do coolie labor, kept in a pighouse, he watched his brother missionaries die. Even when giving a funeral address in a prison camp, he was able to win men to Christ.

The Presswoods returned to Borneo, on November 27, 1945, and Ernie discovered the grave of his successor, who had been bayoneted to death after surrendering to prevent reprisals on the natives. When the Presswoods went up-country, they found that the war had caused divided loyalties, disputes and much backsliding, even some rebuilding of spirit altars.

"Such things were disheartening to Ernie," writes Ruth. But there were repentance, and much hunger.

Nor need Presswood have feared. The horrors of the Pacific War, the disturbances of the War of Independence and the checkered growth of Sukarno's Indonesia could not quench so deep a movement of the Spirit. Over the Sarawak border a great forward movement began in the 1950s, with the Muruts as the spearhead bringing the gospel to other tribes, while the Borneo Evangelical Mission workers translated the Scriptures into the different languages, ran a Bible school and set up their own air service.

Ernie Presswood did not live to see it. At Long Berang, on that first postwar visit of January 1946, a severe bout of sickness convinced him, physically weak from his sufferings as a prisoner, that he must return down stream to the coast at once or die. The river was high, but a legend among the Muruts that natives tried to stop him from traveling is disproved by contemporary letters. On Ernie's 38th birthday the Presswoods set off, with seven boatmen and another passenger carrying a live pig to sell at the market.

Fun on the Rapids

At the first rapids they had to land and crawl among the leeches through the edge of the undergrowth. After that the going was easier. "We continued shooting rapids for several hours and I found it fun," writes Ruth.

At the last and biggest, the boatmen climbed up the mountainside to reconnoiter and reported it safe to negotiate, so they floated out past a big boulder. They were struck by a 10-foot wave. The next capsized them. Ruth could not swim and Ernie grabbed her. They were carried downstream 300 yards, much of it underwater.

They scrambled ashore, safe except for baggage which was nearly all lost, and finally reached the coast after a trying journey wedged among prisoners of war in an overloaded motor boat.

The drenching seriously affected Presswood's shattered constitution. But he had promised to attend a conference across the bay, and though he felt ill and Ruth was sick and unable to accompany him, he kept his word. Pneumonia set in.

On February 1, 1946, he died. His memorial is the vigorous evangelical church in Borneo.